Choose the Perfect Name for Your Baby

CHOOSE THE PERFECT NAME FOR YOUR BABY

SARAH B. PARSONS

LONGMEADOW PRESS

Copyright © 1992 by Longemeadow Press

Published by Longmeadow Press, 201 High Ridge Road,
Stamford, CT 06904. All rights reserved. No part of this book
may be reproduced or utilized in any form or by any means,
electornic or mechanical, including photocopying, recording
or by any information storage and retrieval system, without
permission in writing from the Publisher.

Cover design by Jim McGuire

Interior design by Fritz Metsch

Library of Congress Cataloging-in-Publication Data

Parsons, Sarah B.
    Choose the perfect name for your baby / Sarah B. Parsons.
—1st ed.
      p. cm.
    ISBN: 0-681-41444-8 :
    1. Names, Personal—Dictionaries.   I. Title.
CS2377.P29   1992
929.4′03—dc20   92-10483
                                               CIP

Printed in United States of America

First Edition

0 9 8 7 6 5 4 3 2 1

To Donald Holcombe Parsons and Sarah Angell Parsons,

My Parents,

For giving me a name I have always liked.

Introduction

What could be more exciting during those last few months of your pregnancy than settling down to choose that most enduring of gifts—your child's name?

But wait a minute! It's not so easy. Where to begin? Your head swirls with only the most inappropriate names: your most hated rivals in grade school, the plumber, your father's detested business partner. These aren't the ones that, years ago, you promised yourself would be lovingly recalled for your firstborn. What happened? Where to begin?

Naming "experts" are considered experts because they know lots of names, what they mean, and where they come from. They also know all "the rules" of choosing a name for your baby. But what do they know about you or your baby? And how can the experts and their rules help you before you know a little bit more about yourself, and all those preferences that might lead you to the perfect name for your baby?

Before naming my own children, I read as much as possible about names and naming practices. I wanted to know what all my choices were, so I pored over lists of names. But what really took time was weighing all the special, individual considerations that affected the narrowing down of my personal list. And I found that the "naming experts" didn't discuss the personal considerations involved in choosing the perfect name.

For that reason, I have postponed the rules of name-choosing—perhaps I should call them hints or tips—until later in the book. What follows almost immediately after this introduction is the actual list of names—over ten thousand of them. But before getting to the name list itself I have included a baby name checklist. This checklist is intended to provide you with a customized master list of names that *you* can select from. So before you start choosing names, preferring one variant to another, discarding a third because it rhymes with your last name, find out where *you* really want to begin. Kick off your shoes, get comfortable, and take your time arriving at answers to the following twelve questions. The results will make the task of choosing your baby's name much more personal—as it should be.

■ THE BABY NAME CHECKLIST ■

1. _____ is a name I have always loved. Do I still?
2. Does my religion dictate or prohibit the name I choose for my child?
3. The person in the world, living or dead, whom I most admire is _____ . Is it Mom? Dad? A great movie star?
4. What are the most popular names today? Am I a slave to fashion? Or am I looking for an old standard?
5. Does my baby need a middle name?
6. Do I have a loved and admired relative I want to name the baby after?
7. What was my great-great-grandfather's name? My great-great-grandmother's?
8. What is my baby's birth sign, stone, and flower going to be? Do I care?
9. Who was the winning pitcher in the last game of the 1958 World Series? Does it matter?
10. Do I know the amniocentesis results? If not, should I choose a name that will work for both sexes?
11. Do I want the name to reflect my cultural heritage?
12. Must I choose a name that has been used before, or can I make up my own?

BOYS

BOYS
A

Aaron (Hebrew) Biblical name meaning "high mountain" or "exalted one." Aaron was the brother of Moses and the first high priest of the Jews. Aaron Burr, third U.S. vice president; Aaron Copland, composer. **Aaren, Aarron, Aharon, Ari, Arnie, Arny, Aron, Arron, Erin, Haroun, Ron, Ronnie, Ronny**

Abbott (Arabic) "Father" or, more specifically, "father of the Abbey." Abbie Hoffman, radical activist. **Ab, Abba, Abbe, Abbey, Abbie, Abbot, Abby**

Abdul (Arabic) "Son of" or "servant of." Kareem Abdul-Jabbar, basketball player. **Abdel, Del**

Abel (Hebrew) Biblical name meaning "breath" or "vapor-like." Abel, the second son of Adam and Eve, was murdered by his brother Cain. **Abe, Abele, Abie**

Abelard (Old German) "Noble and resolute." **Abe, Abel, Abelar**

Abner (Hebrew) "Father of light." Abner Doubleday, who is said to have invented baseball. **Ab, Av, Avner, Eb, Ebbie, Ebner**

Abraham (Hebrew) Biblical name meaning "father of the multitude." Abraham, with his wife, Sarah, founded the Hebrew nation. Abraham Lincoln, sixteenth U.S. president. **Abe, Abram, Aram, Avram, Avrom, Bram, Ibrahim**

Ace (Latin) "Unity." **Acey, Asa, Ase**

Acton (Old English) "Town with many oaks." Anne Brontë picked this name for her pseudonym, Acton Bell.

Adair (Scottish Gaelic) "From the oak tree ford."

Adam (Hebrew) Biblical name meaning "man of the red earth." Adam Clayton Powell, Jr., American politician. **Ad, Adamo, Adams, Addam, Addy, Ade, Adey, Adie,**

Addison (Old English) "Son of Adam." **Adamson, Addy**

Adlai (Hebrew) Biblical name meaning "God is my witness." Adlai Stevenson, U.S. politician. **Adalai, Adlay**

Adler (German) "Eagle," implying extraordinary vision of eye and mind. **Adley, Adlie**

Adolph (German) "Noble wolf" or "noble hero." Adolf Hitler, German political leader; Adolphus Busch, chairman of Anheuser-Busch, Inc. **Adolf, Adolfo, Adolphe, Adolphus, Dolf, Dolph**

Adrian (Latin) "Dark one." Several popes took the name, including the only English pope, Adrian IV. **Adriano, Adrien, Hadrian**

Aeneas (Greek) "Praised one." Name of the hero in Virgil's epic poem *The Aeneid*. **Aineas, Eneas**

Ahmad (Arabic) "The most praised." One of the many names used to designate the prophet Muhammad. Ahmet Ertegun, music producer. **Ahmed, Ahmet**

Aidan (Irish Gaelic) "Fire" or "warmth of the home." Aidan Quinn, actor. **Aden, Aeddan, Aiden, Edan**

Aiken (Old English) "Oakenlike," implying strength. **Aikin**

Ainsley (Old English) "From one's own meadow." **Ainslie, Ansley, Anslie**

Alastair (Scottish) Form of Alexander. Alistair Cooke, broadcast journalist. **Alasdair, Alastar, Alasteir, Alistair, Allister, Allistir**

Albert (Old English) "Noble and bright." Albert Camus, French novelist; Albert Einstein, scientist; Albert Finney, British actor. **Al, Albie, Alberto, Albrecht, Bert, Bertie, Berty, Burt, Elbert**

Alcott (Old English) "From the old cottage." **Alcot**

Alden (Old English) "An old friend." **Aldin, Aldwin, Aldwyn, Elden, Eldin**

Aldous (Old German) "Old, wise one." Aldous Huxley, British writer. **Aldis, Aldo, Aldus**

Aldrich (Old English) "Wise, old leader." **Aldric, Aldridge, Alric, Rich, Richie, Richy**

Alexander (Greek) "Defender of men." Made popular throughout the world by Alexander the Great. Alexander Graham Bell, telephone inventor; Alexander Calder, sculptor; Sir Alec Guinness, British actor; Alex Haley, author of *Roots*. **Al, Alastair, Alec, Alejo, Aleksandr, Aleksei, Aleksy, Alex, Alessandro, Alexandre, Alexio, Alexis, Alexius, Alistair, Alister, Alsandair, Sander, Sandy, Sasha, Saunder**

Alfred (Old English) "Elfin or wise counselor." King Alfred the Great of England. Alfred Hitchcock, movie director and producer; Alfred Knopf, book publisher; Alfredo (Al) Pacino, actor. **Al, Alf, Alfie, Alfredo, Fred, Freddie, Fredo**

Algernon (Old French) "One with whiskers," referring to one who is not clean-shaven. **Alger, Algie, Algy, Elgar**

Allan (Irish) "Handsome, harmonious one." Alan Arkin, actor; Allen Ginsberg, "beat" poet; Alan Jay Lerner, lyricist and playwright. **Ailean, Ailin, Alain, Alan, Alano, Allen, Allyn**

Aloysius (Old German) "Illustrious warrior." **Aloys**

Alphonse (Old German) "Of noble estate or family" and "ready for battle." Alphonse (Al) Capone, U.S. gangster; Alphonse D'Amato, U.S. senator from New York State. **Al, Alf, Alfio, Alfons, Alfonso, Alfonzo, Alford, Alfy, Alonso, Alphonsus, Fons, Fonsie, Fonz, Fonzie**

Altman (Old German) "Old, wise man." St. Altman, founded Benedictine Abbey. **Alter, Altmann**

Alvin (Old German) "Noble friend or old friend." **Alva, Alvan, Alven, Alvie, Alvy, Alvyn, Alwyn, Elvin**

Ambrose (Greek) "Immortal one." Ambrose Bierce, American author. **Ambie, Ambroise, Ambros, Amby, Emrys, Brose**

Amadeus (Latin) "One who loves God." Wolfgang Amadeus Mozart, Austrian composer. **Amadeo, Amadis, Amado, Amando**

Amiel (Hebrew) "Leader of my people."

Amory (Old German) "Divine ruler." **Amery, Emery**

Amos (Hebrew) Biblical name meaning "burden bearer." Old Testament prophet. Amos and Andy, comedy team.

Anatole (Greek) "From where the sun rises." **Anatoli, Anatolio, Anatoly, Anotol**

Andrew (Greek) "Manly." The first Apostle, St. Andrew is the patron saint of Scotland. Andrew Jackson, seventh U.S. president. **Anders, André, Andrea, Andreas, Andrej, Andy, Drew, Dru**

Angelo (Greek) "A messenger of God." **Angel, Angell, Angelos, Angelus, Angie**

Angus (Scottish Gaelic) "One with a unique choice." Popular Scottish name. Angus Wilson, writer. **Angie, Ennis, Gus**

Anselm (Old German) "Divine guardian." Most commonly used form of the name today is Ansel as in Ansel Adams, photographer. **Ancel, Ancell, Anse, Ansel, Ansell, Elmo**

Anson (Anglo Saxon) "Son of a nobleman." **Ansen, Hansen, Hanson**

Anthony (Latin) "A priceless one." St. Anthony, patron saint of the poor. Anthony Quinn, British actor; Anton Chekhov, Russian playwright. **Antin, Antoine, Anton, Antone, Antonin, Antonio, Antony, Toni, Tonio, Tony**

Apollo (Greek) "Beautiful, manly one." In classical Greek mythology, Apollo is the sun god. **Apollinare, Apollinaris, Polo**

Archibald (German) "Nobly bold." Archibald MacLeish, Pulitzer Prize-winning poet. **Arch, Archambault, Archer, Archibaldo, Archibold, Archie**

Arden (Latin) "Ardent, fiery." **Ardin**

Ardley (Old English) "From the meadow of the home-lover." **Ardlie, Ardly**

Ardmore (Latin) "One who is more ardent." **Ard, Ardie**

Argus (Greek) "All seeing." **Gus**

Ariel (Hebrew) "Lion of God." **Arel**

Aristotle (Greek) "A great thinker." Aristotle Onassis, Greek shipping magnate; Aristotle (Telly) Savalas, actor. **Ari, Ary**

Arlo (Spanish) "From the fortified hill." Arlo Guthrie, American folk singer. **Carlo, Harlow**

Armand (Old German) "An armed man." Form of Herman. Armand Hammer, U.S. businessman. **Armando, Armin, Armond**

Armstrong (Old English) "Strong of arm," implying one who is strong in battle.

Arnett (Old French) "Like a small eagle." **Arnatt, Arnet**

Arnold (Old German) "One who has the power of an eagle." Arnold Schwarzenegger, actor. **Arnaud, Arnaut, Arne, Arney, Arni, Arnie, Arno, Arny**

Arthur (Irish) "Stonelike" (Welsh) "bear-man." King Arthur, legendary English ruler. Arthur Ashe, tennis player; Arthur Miller, playwright; Art Garfunkel, singer; Arthur Ochs Sulzberger, publisher of *The New York Times*. **Art, Artair, Arte, Arther, Artie, Arturo, Aurtur**

Arvin (Old German) "A friend of the people." Arvin Brown, theater director. **Arvyn**

Asa (Hebrew) "Physician" or "healer." Asa Randolph, U.S. labor leader.

Ashburn (Old English) "From near the ash-tree brook."

Ashford (Old English) "From near the ash-tree ford." **Ford**

Ashley (Old English) "From the ash-tree meadow." Ashley

Wilkes, character in *Gone With the Wind*. Today it's used predominantly as a female name. **Ash, Ashlie**

Ashton (Old English) "From the town of ash-trees." **Ashten**

Athol (Scottish Gaelic) "From Ireland." Athol Fugard, playwright. **Athole, Atholl**

Aubrey (German) "Ruler of the elves." **Alberik, Auberon, Avery, Oberon**

Augustus (Latin) "Venerable one." Used by Roman emperors beginning with Augustus Caesar. Auguste Rodin, sculptor. **Augie, August, Auguste, Augustin, Augustine, Austen, Austin, Gus**

Austin (Latin) Form of Augustus. **Austen, Austyn, Ostin**

Averell (Middle English) "Born in April" (Old English) "boar-warrior." Averell Harriman, U.S. politician. **Av, Ave, Averil, Averill**

Avery (Old English) "A wise counselor." Form of Alfred. **Aubrey**

Axel (Old German) "Father of peace." Axel Stordahl, musical arranger. **Absalom, Axl**

Azariah (Hebrew) Biblical name meaning "one whom God helps." Most frequently used name in the Bible. **Azarias, Azriel**

While the practice of using middle names is relatively new—no one on the *Mayflower* had one—more than 90 percent of Americans today do have a middle name. Often the mother's maiden name is used. Middle names are a nice way to incorporate family names without being reminded of that relative on a day-to-day basis. This is a good time to look at your family tree for ideas.

If you can't settle on a middle name, consider using just an initial. The U.S. armed forces expect you to have one. In fact, if you have no middle initial, they enter NMI (no middle initial) on your records.

Some people are better known by their middle names:

1. Eleanor Rosalynn Carter
2. Stephen Grover Cleveland
3. Alfred Alistair Cooke
4. John Calvin Coolidge
5. Mary Farrah Fawcett
6. William Clark Gable
7. Terence Stephen McQueen
8. James David Niven
9. Olive Marie Osmond
10. Margaret Jane Pauley
11. Charles Robert Redford
12. Anna Eleanor Roosevelt
13. Robert Sargent Shriver
14. Michael Sylvester Stallone
15. George Orson Welles

BOYS
B

Bailey (Old French) "A bailiff or steward." **Bail, Baillie, Baily, Bayley**

Bain (Irish Gaelic) "Fair."

Baird (Irish Gaelic) "Ballad singer." **Bar, Bard, Barr**

Baldwin (Old German) "Bold or courageous friend." **Balduin, Baudoin, Baudouin, Win**

Balfour (Scottish Gaelic) "From the pasture."

Ballard (Old German) "Bold, strong, courageous one."

Bancroft (Old English) "Of the bean field." **Bain, Baine, Bank, Bink, Binky**

Barclay (Old English) Form of Berkeley. **Clay**

Barlow (Old English) "From the bare hill" or "from the boar hill." **Barlie, Barly**

Barnabus (Greek) "Son of prophecy." Modern variant is **Barney** or **Barnaby**.

Barnes (Old English) "Bearlike." **Barny**

Barnett (Old English) "A nobleman." (Old German) Form of Bernard. **Barnet, Barney, Barron**

Barnum (Old English) "Nobleman's home."

Barrett (Old German) "Strong and mighty as a bear." (Middle English) "Argumentative one." Elizabeth Barrett Browning, poet. **Baret**

Barry (Old English) "One who lives near the gate or barrier." Barry Goldwater, U.S. politician; Barry Manilow, singer. **Bari, Barrie, Barris, Bary**

Bartholomew (Hebrew) "One who farms." **Bart, Barth, Bartholome, Bartlett, Bartley, Barton**

Basil (Latin) "Kingly one." **Basile, Basilio, Bayzl, Bazil, Vasili**

Baxter (Old English) "A baker." **Bax**

Bayard (Old English) "Having reddish-brown hair." Bayard Taylor, American essayist. **Bay**

Beal (Old French) "Handsome one." **Beale, Beall**

Beaufort (Old English) "From the beautiful fort." **Beauforte, Boforte**

Beaumont (Old French) "From the beautiful mountain town." **Belmont, Bomonte**

Beauregard, Beau (Old French) "Handsome." Beau Bridges, actor. **Beal, Beale, Bo**

Beck (Middle English) "From near a brook." **Bek**

Bellamy (Old French) "Handsome friend." **Belamy, Bellum**

Benedict (Latin) "Blessed one." Benedict Arnold, revolutionary soldier and traitor; Benito Mussolini, Italian political leader. **Ben, Benedick, Benedicto, Benito, Bennet, Benoit, Bendix, Dick**

Benjamin (Hebrew) Biblical name meaning "son of my right hand." Youngest son of Rachel and Jacob. Benjamin Franklin, inventor; Dr. Benjamin Spock, pediatrician; Bennie Goodman, musician; Ben Hogan, golfer. **Ben, Benj, Benji, Benjie, Bennie, Benny, Jamie**

Bennett (French) "Blessed small one." Bennett Cerf, book publisher. **Benet**

Benson (Hebrew) "Son of Benjamin."

Bentley (Old English) "From the bent-grass clearing." **Bent, Bentlie, Bently, Benton**

Bergen (Scandinavian) "From the hill or mountain." **Berg, Berger, Bergren**

Berkeley (Old English) "From the clearing of birch trees." **Berk, Berkie, Berkley, Berky**

Bernard (Old German) "Brave as a bear." George Bernard Shaw, English writer; Bjorn Borg, tennis player. **Barnard, Barney, Bern, Berne, Bernhard, Bernie, Bjorn**

Berry (Old German) "Bearlike." Berry Gordy, Jr., record producer.

Berthold (Old German) "Brilliant ruler." Bertold Brecht, playwright. **Bert, Bertie, Bertold, Bertoldi**

Bertram (Old English) "Brilliant raven" or (Old French) "Illustrious one." Bert Lahr, actor; Bertrand Russell, British writer. **Bart, Bartram, Bert, Bertie, Bertrand**

Bevan (Welsh) "Son of Evan, youthful one." **Beaven, Beven, Bevon**

Billy (Old German) "Firmly determined guardian." Pet form of William. Billy Crystal, actor; Billy Joel, singer and songwriter; Billy Martin, baseball manager; Bill Murray, comedian. **Bill, Billie**

Bing (Old German) "Of the kettle-shaped hollow." Bing Crosby, entertainer.

Birch (Old English) "Birch treelike," probably referring to the tree's white color. **Birck, Birk, Burch, Burk**

Birney (Old English) "From the island in the brook." **Burney**

Blaine (Irish Gaelic) "Thin one." (Old English) "From near the river's source." **Blane, Blayne**

Blair (Irish Gaelic) "From the plain or flatlands." **Blare**

Blake (Old English) "Pale or light-haired" and "dark one." A name given to someone with extreme coloring, whether it be light or dark. Blake Edwards, movie producer and director. **Blakeley**

Blaze (Latin) "One who stutters." Blaise Pascal, seventeenth-century French philosopher. **Blaise, Blase, Blayze**

Bob (Old German) "Brilliant warrior." Pet form of Robert. Bob Hope, entertainer; Bob Seger, rock singer; Bobby Orr, hockey player. **Bobbie, Bobby**

Boden (Old French) "A messenger." **Bodin**

Bogart (Old German) "One who is strong with a bow." **Bo, Bogey, Bogie**

Bonar (Old French) "Kind, courteous one." A shortened form of the word debonnaire. **Bonnar**

Bond (Old English) "One who binds or tills the soil." **Bonde, Bondon, Bonds**

Booker (English) "The book," referring to the Bible. Booker T. Washington, educator.

Boone (Old French) "One who is good and bounteous." **Boon**

Booth (Middle English) "From the hut." Booth Tarkington, writer. **Boot, Boothe**

Bordon (Old English) "From the cottage in the boar valley." **Bordan, Bordin**

Boris (Russian) "Glorious warrior." Boris Becker, tennis player; Boris Pasternak, Nobel Prize-winning author of *Dr. Zhivago*. **Bobo, Bory**

Boswell (Old French) "From the estate in the forest." **Bosley**

Bowie (Irish Gaelic) "Small fighter." **Bow, Bowan, Boyd**

Boyce (Old French) "From the woods." **Boise**

Bradburn (Old English) "From the broad brook or stream." **Braden**

Bradford (Old English) "From near the broad river crossing." **Brad, Ford**

Bradley (Old English) "From the broad meadow or clearing." **Brad, Bradly, Lee, Leigh**

Bradshaw (Old English) "From the broad, virginal forest." **Brad, Shaw**

Brady (Irish Gaelic) "High-spirited one." or (Old English) "from the wide, broad island." **Brad**

Bram (Irish Gaelic) "Raven."

Brandon (Old English) "From the settlement on a bramble-covered hill." **Bran, Brand, Branden, Brandy, Brant, Branton**

Brendan (Celtic) "Princely one." (Irish Gaelic) "Like a little raven." Brendan Gill, American writer. **Bren, Brenden**

Brent (Old English) "From the steep hill." **Brenton**

Brett (Latin) "A Briton; one from Brittany." Brett Easton Ellis, American novelist. **Bret**

Brewster (Middle English) "A brewer." **Brew, Bruce**

Brian (Irish Gaelic) "Strong one." Bryant Gumbel, TV journalist. **Brien, Brion, Bryan, Bryant, Bryon**

Brice (Welsh) "Speckled one." (Celtic) "Quick-moving one." **Brick, Bryce, Brys**

Brigham (Middle English) "From the town near the bridge." Brigham Young, Mormon leader. **Brigg, Briggs**

Brock (Old English) "Badger." Brock Yates, automotive journalist and writer.

Broderick (Middle English) "From the broad or wide ridge." (Scandinavian) "A brother." (Welsh) "Son of Roderick." **Brod, Broddie, Broddy, Broder, Broderic, Derick, Rick, Rickie, Ricky**

Brodie (Irish Gaelic) "From the ditch." Probably referring to a person who dug a ditch for irrigation purposes. A Scottish clan name. **Brodi, Brody**

Bromley (Old English) "From the broom or bramble meadow." **Brom, Bronley, Lee, Leigh**

Bronson (Old English) "Son of one who is dark-skinned." **Bron, Bronnie, Bronny, Son, Sonny**

Brook (Middle English) "One who lives near a brook." Brooks Atkinson, journalist; Brooks Adams, historian. **Brooke, Brooks**

Bruce (Old French) "One who lives in the thicket." Bruce Jenner, Olympic athlete; Bruce Dern, Bruce Lee, and Bruce Willis, actors; Bruce Springsteen, singer and songwriter. **Brucie**

Bruno (Italian) "Brown-haired." Bruno Bettelheim, child psychologist.

Buck (Old English) "Like a male deer," referring to someone who is robust and manly. **Buckie, Buckley, Bucky**

Buckminster (Old English) "A preacher." R. Buckminster Fuller, innovative engineer.

Buddy (English) "A friend." Buddy Ebsen and Buddy Hackett, actors. **Bud, Budd, Buddie**

Burgess (Middle English) "Member of the town." Burgess Meredith, actor. **Burg, Burr**

Burke (Old French) "From the fortress or stronghold." **Berk, Berke, Birk, Birke, Burk**

Burl (Old English) "One who serves the wine; the cupbearer." Burl Ives, entertainer. **Byrle**

Burton (Old English) "From the fortress on the hill." Burt Bacharach, composer; Burt Lancaster and Burt Reynolds, actors. **Bert, Berton, Burt, Butch**

Byron (Old French) "From the country estate or cottage." Byron Allen, comedian. **Biron, Byran**

BOYS
C

Caesar (Latin) "Long-haired one." It is the name of so many Roman emperors that it has come to mean "emperor or ruler." Cesar Romero, actor. **Cesar, Cesare, Cesaro**

Cain (Hebrew) Biblical name meaning "a spear." Cain, the first son of Adam and Eve, murdered his brother Abel in a fit of jealousy. **Caine**

Calder (Old English) "From the clear stream." **Cal**

Caldwell (Old English) "One who lives by the cool, clear stream or well." **Cal, Wells**

Caleb (Hebrew) Biblical name meaning "doglike one," referring to a strong fidelity and devotion to God. **Cal, Cale, Kale, Kaleb**

Calhoun (Celtic) "Clearheaded warrior." (Irish Gaelic) "From the clearing in the forest."

Calum (Latin) "Dovelike," referring to the dove as a symbol for the peace and purity of the Holy Spirit. **Caley, Cally, Colm, Colom, Columba**

Calvert (Old English) "Calfherder." **Calbert**

Calvin (Latin) "Small, bald one." Calvin Coolidge, thirtieth U.S. president. **Cal, Calvino, Kalvin, Vin, Vinnie, Vinny**

Camden (Scottish Gaelic) "From the winding, crooked valley." **Cam, Camdon**

Cameron (Scottish Gaelic) "One with a crooked nose." A Scottish clan name. Cameron MacIntosh, theatrical producer. **Cam, Cammie, Cammy**

Campbell (Scottish Gaelic) "One with a crooked mouth." A Scottish clan name. **Cam, Camp, Campy**

Carey (Old Welsh) "One who lives in or by the castle." Cary Grant, actor. **Care, Cary**

Carl (Old German) "A farmer" or "man who lives in the

country." Carl Bernstein, journalist; Carl Sandburg, poet.
Car, Carle, Karl

Carlin (Irish Gaelic) "A small champion." **Carlie, Carling, Carly**

Carlisle (Old English) "From the walled city with the castle." **Carl, Carlie, Carly, Carlyle**

Carlos (Spanish) Form of Charles meaning "manly." Carlos Santana, rock musician. **Carlo**

Carmichael (Scottish Gaelic) "Friend of St. Michael," or "From Michael's fortress." **Carmie, Carmy, Michael**

Carmine (Latin) "Songlike one" or "crimson-colored."

Carney (Irish Gaelic) "Victorious one." **Carny, Karney, Kearney**

Carr (Scandinavian) "From the marsh or wetlands." **Karr, Kerr**

Carroll (Irish Gaelic) "Champion." Carroll O'Connor, actor. **Carey, Carrol, Cary, Caryl**

Carson (Old English) "Son of the marsh dweller."

Carter (Old English) "A driver of carts." **Cart, Cartland**

Carver (Old English) "Wood carver."

Casey (Irish Gaelic) "Brave." Casey Stengel, baseball manager. **Case, Cayse**

Casimir (Slavic) "One who proclaims peace." The name of many Polish kings in the Middle Ages. **Casimire, Casper, Cass, Cassie, Cassy, Kasper, Kazimir**

Caspar (Persian) "Keeper of the treasure." Caspar Weinberger, U.S. politician. **Casper, Cass, Gaspar, Gaspard, Gasper, Jasper, Kaspar, Kasper**

Cassidy (Irish Gaelic) "Curly-haired" or "clever one." **Cass, Cassie, Cassy**

Cassius (Latin) "Vain one." Cassius Clay, the heavyweight boxing champion who changed his name to Muhammad Ali. **Cash, Cass, Cassian, Cassus, Caz**

Cecil (Old Welsh) "Sixth one." (Latin) "One who is unable to see." Ironically, the name of photographer Cecil Beaton. **Cece, Cecile, Cecilio, Cecilius**

Cedric (Welsh) "A leader in battle" or "of the bounty." Name of the boy hero in Frances Hodgson Burnett's novel *Little Lord Fauntleroy*. **Cedrick, Cedrych, Cerdic**

Chad (Old English) "Warrior." Pet form of Charles. Chad Everett, actor. **Chadd**

Chadwick (Old English) "From the town of the warrior." **Wick**

Chaim (Hebrew) "Life." Chaim Weizmann, first president of the State of Israel; Chaim Potok, author. **Hyam, Hyman, Hymie, Mannie, Manny**

Chalmers (Scottish Gaelic) "Head of the house or estate." **Chalmer**

Chandler (Old French) "Candlemaker, provider of light." **Chan, Chane, Chaney, Cheney**

Channing (Old French) "A clergyman or canon." **Chan, Chanely**

Charles (Old German) "A strong man." Charles de Gaulle, president of France; Charles Windsor, prince of Wales; Charles Dickens, English writer. **Charlie, Charley, Chas, Chick, Chip, Chuck, Chuckie**

Charleton (Old English) "From Charles's estate or town." Charlton Heston, actor. **Carl, Carleton, Carlton, Charlton**

Chase (Old French) "A hunter."

Chauncey (Middle English) "An official of the church; chancellor." **Chance, Chancey, Chaunce, Chauncy**

Chester (Old English) "From the fortress." Chester Alan Arthur, twenty-first U.S. president; Chet Huntley, TV journalist. **Ches, Cheston, Chet**

Chevalier (French) "A knight." **Chev, Chevy**

Chico (Spanish) "A Frenchman." Pet form of Francisco. Chico Marx, one of the Marx brothers.

Christian (Greek) "A follower of Christ." Christian Dior, fashion designer; Kit Carson, frontiersman; Christian Slater, actor. **Chretien, Chris, Christ, Christiano, Christy, Kit, Kitt, Kris, Krispin, Kristian**

Christopher (Greek) "One who carries Christ in his heart." Christopher Columbus, Italian explorer who discovered America; Christopher Marlowe, playwright; Christopher Robin, name of A. A. Milne's son and character in his stories *Winnie the Pooh;* Christopher Reeve, actor. **Chris, Christoffer, Christoforo, Christoph, Christophe, Christophorus, Cris, Cristo, Cristoforo, Cristos, Kristo, Kristofer, Kristoforo, Kristos**

Cian (Irish Gaelic) "Ancient one." **Kean, Keane**

Cicero (Latin) "A chick-pea." Name of the great Roman orator and statesman who died in 43 B.C. He is said to be named for his family's bountiful field of chick-peas. **Cece, Cero, Rory**

Cid (Spanish) "A lord." **Cyd**

Claiborne (Old English) "From the clay-bottom brook" or "born of the earth." **Claiborn, Clayborne, Claybourne**

Clarence (Latin) "Illustrious one." Clarence Darrow, famous attorney; Clarence Thomas, U.S. Supreme Court justice. **Clare, Clair, Clarrie, Clarance**

Clark (Latin) "A clerk or scholar." Clark Gable, actor; Clark Kent, Superman's civilian name. **Clarke, Clerc, Clerk**

Claude (Latin) "One who is lame." Claude Monet, impressionist painter; Claude Pepper, U.S. senator. **Claudian, Claudio, Claudius, Claus**

Clay (Old English) "From the land of claylike soil." **Claigh, Claighton, Clayton, Cleighton**

Clement (Latin) Biblical name meaning "merciful one." Clement E. Moore, writer. **Clem, Clemens, Clemente, Clemmie, Clemmy, Klem, Klement**

Cleveland (Old English) "From the land full of cliffs." Cleveland Amory, writer. **Cleaveland, Cleavland, Cleve, Clevie, Clevon, Clevy**

Clifford (Old English) "From the steep river crossing." Cliff Robertson, actor. **Cliff, Clifton**

Clint (Old English) "From the settlement near the cliff." Clint Eastwood, actor. **Clinton**

Clive (Old English) "From the cliff." Clive Barnes, drama critic. **Cleve, Clyve**

Clune (Irish Gaelic) "From the open land." **Cluney, Cluny**

Clyde (Scottish Gaelic) "One who is heard from on high." (Welsh) "Warm one." Name comes from the River Clyde in Scotland. Clyde Barrow, of the famous bank robber team Bonnie and Clyde. **Cly, Clyd, Clywd**

Cody (English) Meaning unknown. **Codi, Codie**

Colby (Old English) "From the coal town." **Colburn, Colburt**

Cole (Greek) "Of the victorious ones." Pet form of Nicolas. Cole Porter, American songwriter; Coleman Young, mayor of Detroit. **Colan, Coleman, Colman**

Colin (Irish Gaelic) "One who is young and virile." (Greek) "Of the victorious one." A pet form of Nicholas. Colin Powell, chairman, Joint Chiefs of Staff. **Cailean, Colan, Cole, Collin**

Collier (Old English) "A miner." **Colier, Collayer, Collis, Collyer, Colyer**

Colter (Old English) "One who herds colts." **Colt, Colton**

Conall (Scottish Gaelic) "A courageous warrior." **Conal, Conlan, Conley, Conlin, Conn, Connel, Konal**

Conan (Irish Gaelic) "Wise, heroic one." Conan the Barbarian, comic strip character; Sir Arthur Conan Doyle, British writer and creator of Sherlock Holmes. **Conant, Conon, Connor**

Conrad (Old German) "Brave, wise counselor." Conrad Aiken, writer; Conrad Hilton, hotel executive. **Con, Conney, Conrade, Conrado, Cort, Konrad, Kort**

Conroy (Irish Gaelic) "Wise one." **Conn, Conney, Conny, Roy**

Constantine (Latin) "One who is constant and true." Constantine the Great, Roman emperor of the fourth century; Constant Tryon, French landscape painter. **Constant, Constantin, Constantino, Costa, Konstantin, Konstantine, Konstantyn, Kosta**

Conway (Irish Gaelic) "Hound of the plain."

Cooper (Old English) "A producer of barrels" **Coop**

Corbett (Old French) "Raven-colored hair." **Corbet, Corbin, Corby**

Corcoran (Irish Gaelic) "One with a red complexion." **Corcie, Corcy, Cork, Corky**

Cordell (Old French) "Ropemaker." **Cord**

Corey (Irish Gaellic) "From the ravine." Corey Allen, actor. **Correy, Cory, Corry**

Cormack (Irish Gaelic) "A chariot driver." **Cormac, Cormag, Cormick**

Cornelius (Latin) "Carrier of the war horn." A Roman clan name. Cornelius (Chevy) Chase, comedian; Cornelius Vanderbilt, U.S. railroad tycoon. **Corey, Cornall, Cornelio, Cornell, Cornelus, Cory, Neal**

Cort (Old German) "Bold one." (Scandinavian) "One who is short." **Cortie, Court, Kort**

Corwin (Old French-Old English) "A friend full of heart."

Cosmo (Greek) "One who is in harmony with his surroundings." Cosimo de'Medici, chief patron of the Italian Renaissance. **Cosme, Cosimo**

Courtland (Old English) "From the court land." **Courtley**

Courtney (Old French) "From the estate or court." **Cort, Court, Courtnay, Curt**

Cowan (Irish Gaelic) "From the hollow on the hillside" and possibly "a twin." **Coe**

Craig (Scottish Gaelic) "From the crags." **Craggy, Creggie, Creig**

Crandall (Old English) "From the valley of cranes." **Cran, Crandell, Cranley, Cranston**

Crawford (Old English) "From the crow's ford." **Craw, Crow, Ford**

Creighton (Old English) "From the settlement bounded by the crags." **Creigh, Creight, Crichton**

Crispin (Latin) "Curly-haired one." St. Crispin, third-century patron saint of shoemakers. **Crispian, Crispinus**

Cromwell (Old English) "From near the winding stream." **Wells**

Crosby (Scandinavian) "From near the public cross." **Cross, Crosbey, Crosbie**

Cullen (Irish Gaelic) "Young, handsome one." **Cull, Cullan, Culley, Cullin, Cully**

Culver (Old English) "Dovelike one," referring to peacefulness. **Colver, Cullie, Cully**

Curran (Irish Gaelic) "Heroic one." **Curren, Currey, Currin, Curry**

Curtis (Old French) "One who is courteous." **Curt, Curtice, Curtiss, Kurtis**

Cutler (Old English) "One who makes knives." **Cutley, Cuttie, Cutty**

Cyprian (Greek) "From Cyprus." **Cipriano**

Cyrano (Greek) "One who is from Cyrene." Cyrano de Bergerac, seventeeth-century soldier-poet who is the hero of Rostand's classical tale.

Cyril (Greek) "Of the lord." **Cirillo, Cirilo, Cy, Cyrill, Cyrille, Cyrillus**

Cyrus (Persian) "Sunlike." Cyrus the Great, sixth-century Persian king. Cyrus Vance, U.S. secretary of state. **Ciro, Cy, Russ**

BOYS
D

Dacey (Irish Gaelic) "From the South." **Dace, Dacy**

Dag (Scandinavian) "Of the day." Popular name in Norway. Dag Hammarskjöld, former secretary general of the United Nations.

Dagan (Hebrew) "Of the earth." Name of the Babylonian god of the earth. **Dagon, Dagwood**

Dale (Old English) "From the valley or dale." Popular name in Australia. Dale Carnegie, author and lecturer. **Dael, Daley, Dali, Dalton, Daly, Dayle**

Dallas (Irish Gaelic) "Wise, gentle one." (Old English) "From the estate in the valley." **Dal, Dallan, Dallin, Dalton**

Damian (Greek) "One who is gentle or tame." Damon Knight, science-fiction writer; St. Damien, patron saint of physicians. **Dame, Damen, Damiano, Damien, Damon**

Dana (Scandinavian) "From Denmark." Traditionally a male name but now being used by females. Dana Carvey, comedian. **Dain, Dane**

■ BEGIN AT THE END ■

Your child's surname is the only name you know for certain. So it's the perfect starting point in your name search. Make sure the name you select works with your last name.

If your last name is Pickleheimer, concentrate on more concise, simpler names, such as Amy or John. If, however, your last name is Smith, you might consider a more unusual first name, such as Winona or Paxton.

Daniel (Hebrew) Biblical name meaning "God is my judge." Daniel Boone, American pioneer; Daniel Defoe, author of *Robinson Crusoe;* Dan Aykroyd, actor and comedian; Dan Rather, broadcast journalist; Danny Thomas, entertainer. **Dan, Dannie, Danny**

Dante (Latin) "Enduring one." Dante Alighieri, medieval poet; Dante Gabriel Rosetti, American poet.

Darby (Irish Gaelic) "A free man." (Norwegian) "From the estate full of deer." **Darbee, Derby**

Darcy (Irish Gaelic) "Dark one." (Old French) "From the castle or fortress." **Darce, Darcey, D'Arcy, Darsey, Darsy**

Darius (Persian) "One who excels at maintaining and managing his holdings." Name of many ancient Persian kings. **Dare, Dario, Derry**

Darren (Irish Gaelic) "Great one." Darren McGavin, actor. **Daren, Darin, Daron, Darrin, Derron**

Darryl (Old French) "Dear one." Daryl Hall, rock singer; Darryl Strawberry, baseball player. **Darrel, Darrell, Darrill, Daryl, Derril**

Darwin (Old English) "Dear friend." **Darwyn, Derwin**

David (Hebrew) Biblical name meaning "the beloved one." Name of the greatest king of Israel. Also the patron saint of Wales. David Brinkley, broadcast journalist; David Hockney, British artist; David Letterman, TV personality; David O. Selznick, movie producer. **Dave, Davey, Davie, Davidson, Davin, Davis, Davon, Dawson**

Dayton (Middle English) "From the bright, friendly town." **Dayt**

Deacon (Greek) "Messenger."

Dean (Latin) "Schoolmaster." (Old English) "From the valley." Dean Martin, entertainer. **Deane, Dene, Dino**

Delaney (Irish Gaelic) "One who is descended from the challenger." **Del, Delain, Delainey, Dell, Lane**

Delmar (Latin/Spanish) "From near the sea." Delmore Schwartz, American poet. **Delmer, Delmor, Delmore**

Demetrius (Greek) "Of or belonging to Demeter, the Greek goddess of fertility. **Demetre, Demetrio, Demitri, Dimitri**

Denby (Scandinavian) "From the settlement of Danes." **Danby, Den, Dennie, Denny**

Denholm (Scandinavian) "Home of the Danes." **Denholme**

Dennis (Greek) "Of the god Dionysus" (the god of wine). St. Denis, patron saint of Paris. Dennis Hopper, Dennis Quaid, and Dennis Weaver, actors. **Den, Denis, Dennet, Denney, Dennison, Denys, Dion, Ennis**

Denton (Old English) "From the town in the valley."

Denver (Old English) "From the Dane's crossing place."

Derek (Old German) "Ruler of the people." Derek Jacobi, British stage actor. **Darrick, Deric, Derick, Derik, Derrick, Derrik, Deryck, Dirk**

Dermot (Irish Gaelic) "A free man." **Dermott, Mott**

Desmond (Irish Gaelic) "Descended from a man from South Munster." Desi Arnaz, Jr., entertainer. **Des, Desi, Desmund, Desy**

Devin (Irish Gaelic) "A poet." **Devon**

Dewey (Welsh) "Beloved." A form of David. **Dewi, Dewy**

Dewitt (Flemish) "Blond one." **DeWitt, Dwight, Wit, Witt, Wittie, Witty**

Dexter (Latin) "Right-handed." (Old English) "One who dyes fabric." **Deck, Dex**

Diego (Spanish) "A supplanter." Form of James. Diego Segui, baseball player. **Diogo**

Digby (Old English) "Settlement near a ditch."

Dillon (Irish Gaelic) "Faithful friend." (Old Welsh) "From the sea," referring to the ancient Welsh god of the sea. Dylan Thomas, poet; Dylan McDermott, actor. **Dillan, Dylan**

Dion (Greek) Form of Dionysus. Dion DeMucci, singer who formed the group Dion and the Belmonts. **Dione, Dyon**

Dixon (Old English) "Son of Dick." **Dix, Dixen**

Dominic (Latin) "The lord," probably referring to someone born on Sunday, the Lord's Day. St. Dominic, founder of the Dominican order of preachers; Dominick Dunne, writer. **Dom, Domenic, Domingo, Dominick, Nick**

Donahue (Irish Gaelic) "Dark warrior." **Don, Donnie, Donny, Donohue**

Donald (Irish Gaelic) "Mighty world ruler." Scottish clan name. Don Ameche, Don Johnson, and Donald Sutherland, actors; Donny Osmond, singer. **Don, Donal, Donall, Donnie, Donny**

Donato (Latin) "A gift from God." The marquis de Sade's given name was Donatien. **Donat, Donatien, Donatio, Donatius**

Donnelly (Irish Gaelic) "One who is brave and dark." **Donnell**

Donovan (Irish Gaelic) "Dark warrior." Donovan Leitch, popular singer. **Donavan, Van**

Dorian (Greek) "Gift from the sea." Dorian Grey is the hero of Oscar Wilde's novel *The Picture of Dorian Grey.* **Dore, Doren, Dorey, Dorie, Dorien, Doron, Dorrien, Dory**

Douglas (Scottish Gaelic) "From the dark or black waters." Scottish clan name. Douglas Fairbanks, Sr. and Jr., actors; Douglas MacArthur, U.S. general. **Doug, Dougie, Douglass, Dugald, Duggie**

Doyle (Irish Gaelic) "Black or dark stranger." **Dougal**

Drake (Middle English) "Dragonlike" or "owner of the 'sign of the Dragon' Inn." **Drayke**

Drew (English) "Manly." Short form of Andrew. Drew Middleton, journalist. **Dru**

Dryden (Old English) "From the dry meadow." **Dry, Drydan, Drydon**

Duane (Irish Gaelic) "Small and dark." Duane Allman, rock singer. **Dwain, Dwane, Dwayne**

Dudley (Old English) "From the people's meadow." Dudley Moore, actor. **Dudd, Dudly**

Duke (Old French) "A noble duke." Originally a form of Marmeduke. Duke Ellington, jazz singer.

Duncan (Scottish Gaelic) "Dark-skinned warrior." Duncan Phyfe, furnituremaker. **Dun, Dunc, Duncky, Dune, Dunky, Dunn**

Dunstan (Old English) "From the dark, stony hill." St. Dunstan, tenth-century archbishop of Canterbury.

Durant (Latin) "Enduring one." **Durand, Durante**

Durwin (Anglo Saxon) "Good friend." **Win**

Dustin (Old German) "Valiant fighter." (Old English) "From the dusty place." Dustin Hoffman, actor; Dusty Baker, baseball player. **Dust, Dustan, Dustie, Dustine, Dusty**

Dwight (Dutch) "Blond or white-haired." Dwight D. Eisenhower, thirty-fourth U.S. president.

BOYS
E

Earl (Old English) "Wise." (Old German) "Noble." Former title of nobility now used as a first name. Earl Warren, chief justice of the United States; Erle Stanley Gardner, author of the *Perry Mason* mysteries; Errol Flynn, actor. Earl Weaver, baseball manager. **Earle, Erl, Erle, Errol, Erroll, Rollo**

Eaton (Old English) "From the estate near the river."

Ebenezer (Hebrew) Biblical place name meaning "stone of help." Ebenezer Scrooge, the stingy protagonist in Charles Dickens's novel *A Christmas Carol*. **Ebbe, Eben, Ebeneser**

Eberhard (Old German) "Brave as a wild boar." **Eberhardt, Eberhart**

Edel (Old German) "One who is noble." **Edelmar**

Edison (Old English) "Son of Edward." **Edson**

Edgar (Old English) "Prosperous spearman." Edgar Allan Poe, writer; J. Edgar Hoover, director of the FBI. **Ed, Eddie, Eddy, Edgard, Ned, Ted**

Edmond (Old English) "Prosperous protector." Edmund Muskie, U.S. secretary of state; Edmund Wilson, literary critic and writer. **Eamon, Ed, Edmon, Edmund, Ned, Ted, Teddy**

Edsel (Old English) "From the wealthy man's estate." Edsel Ford, automotive chief executive. **Etzel**

Edward (Old English) "Guardian of one's property or wealth." The name of many English kings. Edward Kennedy, U.S. senator; Edvard Munch, Norwegian painter; Eddie Murphy, comedian and actor. **Ed, Eddie, Eddy, Edouard, Eduardo, Edvard, Ewart, Ned, Ted**

Edwin (Old English) "Prosperous friend." **Edlin, Edwyn**

Egan (Irish Gaelic) "Little, fiery one." (Old German) "One with a pointed sword." **Egon**

Eisner (Hebrew) "One who laughs." **Eise, Eisler**

Eldred (Old English) "Old, wise counsel." Eldridge Cleaver, political activist. **Aldred, Elden, Elder, Eldrid, Eldridge**

Eli (Hebrew) Biblical name meaning "the Lord is God." Eli Whitney, American inventor; Elia Kazan, director. **Eleazar, Elia, Elias, Eliezer, Elihu, Elijah, Ellis, Ely**

Ellery (Latin-Greek) "One who speaks cheerfully." Ellery Queen, fictional detective. **Ellary, Ellerey**

Elliot (Hebrew) "One who believes that God is our lord." Elliot Gould, actor. **Elliott, Eliot**

Ellison (Old English) "Son of Ellis or Elijah." **Elson**

Ellsworth (Old English) "Of the nobleman's estate." Ellsworth Kelly, artist. **Ellard, Elsworth**

Elmer (Old English) "Well-known, famous." (Old German) "Protector." Elmore Leonard, writer. **Elmo, Elmore**

Elroy (Old French) "A king." Elroy Hirsch, athlete. **Roy**

Elston (Old English) "Noble one's town." **Elsdon**

Elton (Old English) "From the old town." Elton John, singer and songwriter. **Eldon**

Elvis (Scandinavian) "All-wise one." Elvis Presley and Elvis Costello, singers. **Alvis, El**

Elwood (Old English) "From the old wood or forest." Elwin B. (E. B.) White, humorist. **Ellwood, Elwin, Woody**

Emery (Old German) "Industrious ruler." **Emerson, Emmery, Emory**

Emil (Latin) "One who flatters." Emilio Pucci, fashion designer. **Emile, Emilio, Emlen, Emlin, Emlyn**

Emmanuel (Hebrew) Biblical name meaning "God is with us." **Eman, Emanuel, Immanuel, Mannie, Manny, Manuel**

Emmett (Old German) "Industrious one." Emmett Kelly, famous circus clown. **Emmet, Emmit, Emmot**

Englebert (Old German) "One as bright as an angel." Engelbert Humperdinck, singer. **Bert, Engelbert, Ingelbert, Inglebert**

Enoch (Hebrew) Biblical name meaning "one with experience and dedication." Name of the son of Cain. **Enock**

Enos (Hebrew) Biblical name meaning "one of mankind." Enos is the son of Seth and grandson of Adam. Enos Slaughter, baseball player.

Ephraim (Hebrew) Biblical name meaning "one who is fruitful." Ephraim was the second son of Joseph. Efrem Zimbalist, Jr., actor. **Efram, Efrem, Ephrem, Ephrim**

Erastus (Greek) "Well loved and loving." St. Erasmus is the patron saint of sailors. **Erasmus, Eraste, Ras, Rastus**

Erdman (German) "A man of the earth." **Erdmann, Hartman**

Eric (Scandinavian) "Ruler of all." Eric Clapton, rock musician; Erich Fromm, psychoanalyst; Eric Heiden, U.S. speed skater; Erich Segal, author of *Love Story.* **Eero, Erich, Erick, Erik, Rick, Ricky**

Erhard (Old German) "Honorable, brave one." **Erhardt, Erhart**

Erland (Scandinavian) "A foreigner." **Erlend**

Ernest (Old English) "One who is earnest." Ernest Borgnine, actor; Ernest Hemingway, writer; Ernie Kovacs, 1950s TV personality. **Ernesto, Ernie, Ernst**

Erskine (Scotch Gaelic) "From the height of the cliff." **Kin, Kinnie, Kinny**

Erwin (Old German) "An honorable friend." **Irwin**

Esau (Hebrew) Biblical name meaning "covered with hair." Esau is Jacob's twin brother.

Esmond (Old English) "Graceful, handsome protector." **Esmen**

Este (Italian) "One from the East." Este Kefauver, U.S. senator. **Estes**

Ethan (Hebrew) "One who is firm, steadfast." Ethan Allen, American revolutionary leader; *Ethan Frome,* novel by Edith Wharton. **Etan, Ethe**

Eugene (Greek) "Well-born." The name of four popes. Eugene McCarthy, U.S. senator; Eugene O'Neill, American playwright. **Eugen, Eugenio, Gene**

Eustace (Greek) "Steadfast." (Latin) "Rich in corn." **Eustis, Stacy**

Evan (Welsh) "A young warrior." Form of John. **Evin, Evyn, Owen**

Evelyn (Old French) "Ancestor of." Evelyn Waugh, English writer. **Evelin, Evelyne**

Everett (Old English) "Strong and brave as a boar." **Eberhard, Everard, Evered, Eward, Ewart**

Everton (Old English) "From a boar farm." **Evers, Evert**

Ezekiel (Hebrew) Biblical name meaning "one whom God strengthens." **Ezechiel, Haskel, Heskel, Zeke**

Ezra (Hebrew) Biblical name meaning "helper." Ezra Pound, poet. **Azariah, Azur, Esdras, Esra, Ezer, Ezri**

BOYS
F

Fabian (Latin) "One who grows beans." **Fabe, Faber, Fabi, Fabiano, Fabien, Fabio**

Fagen (Irish Gaelic) "Small, fiery one." **Fagin**

Fairfax (Old English) "Fair-haired one." **Fair, Fax, Faxie, Faxy**

Farkas (Yiddish) "Wolflike." **Farkie, Farky**

Farley (Old English) "From the sheep meadow." **Fairfax, Fairlay, Farlay, Farlee, Farly, Lee, Leigh**

Farrell (Irish Gaelic) "Courageous, heroic one." **Farr, Farrar, Farrel, Farris, Ferrell, Ferris**

Faust (Latin) "Lucky one." **Faustus**

Felix (Latin) "Happy or fortunate one." Felix Rohayton, financier; Felix Unger, from the TV show *The Odd Couple*. **Fee, Felicio, Feliks**

Fenton (Old English) "From the estate or farm near the marsh." **Fenn**

Ferdinand (Old German) "Bold adventurer." Ferdinand the Great, emperor of Spain; Ferdinand Marcos, Filipino political leader; Ferdinand Porshe, German automotive engineer. **Ferd, Ferdie, Ferdinando, Fernando, Hernando**

Fergus (Irish Gaelic) Form of Ferdinand. **Feargus, Fergie**

Ferrand (Old French) "One with iron-colored hair or an iron temperment." **Farrand, Farrant, Ferrant**

Fidel (Latin) "Faithful one." Fidel Castro, Cuban leader. **Fidele, Fidelio, Fido**

Fielding (Old English) "From the field." **Fee, Field**

Filbert (Old English) "Bright, brilliant one." **Filberto, Phil, Philbert**

Filmore (Old English) "Famous one." **Fillmore, Filmer, Phil**

Finian (Irish Gaelic) "White, fair one." **Finn, Finnian, Fionnan, Fiontan**

Finley (Irish Gaelic) "Fair-haired hero." Popular Scottish name. **Findley, Finlay**

Fiorello (Italian) "Like a little flower," referring to the way it flourishes. Fiorello LaGuardia, American lawyer and politician. **Fio, Fiorenzo**

Fiske (Middle English) "One who sells fish."

Fitzgerald (Old English) "Son of the mighty spearman." **Fitz, Gerald, Gerry, Jerry**

■ WATCH THOSE INITIALS ■

In some circles, it is considered good luck if one's initials form a word. However, Frances Ann Taylor (FAT) doesn't feel so lucky. And Strattford Osgood Brown's parents may call him Stratt, but the kids at school call him SOB. So, if the initials of the name you've chosen form a word, like COW, SAP, TIT or ZIT, you can be sure that it will be brought to your child's attention at least a trillion times.

There are, however, people who choose to be known by their initials. Do you know what names these people's initials stand for?

1. P.T. Barnum	(Phineas Taylor)
2. E.E. Cummings	(Edward Estlin)
3. W.E.B. Du Bois	(William Edward Burghardt)
4. T.S. Eliot	(Thomas Stearns)
5. W.C. Fields	(William Claude)
6. E.M. Forster	(Edward Morgan)
7. H.R. Haldeman	(Harry Robert)
8. D.H. Lawrence	(David Herbert)
9. J.C. Penney	(James Cash)
10. R.J. Reynolds	(Richard Joshua)
11. J.D. Salinger	(Jerome David)
12. O.J. Simpson	(Orenthal James)
13. B.F. Skinner	(Burrhus Frederic)
14. J.R.R. Tolkien	(John Ronald Reuel)
15. H.G. Wells	(Herbert George)

Fitzhugh (Old English) "Son of the intelligent man." **Fitz, Hugh**

Fitzpatrick (Old English) "Son of a nobleman." **Fitz, Pat, Patrick**

Fitzroy (Old French) "Son of a king." **Fitz, Roy**

Flann (Irish Gaelic) "Ruddy-skinned one." **Flannan**

Flavian (Latin) "Golden-haired." **Flavia, Flavio**

Fleming (Old English) "A Flemish or Dutch man." **Flem, Flemming**

Fletcher (Old French) "One who makes or sells arrows." Fletcher Knebel, novelist. **Fletch, Pfeil, Pfeiler, Pheil, Pheyl**

Flint (Old English) "From near the brook." **Flynt**

Florian (Latin) "Flowering or flourishing." **Florent, Florentin, Florentino, Flory**

Floyd (Old English) "Gray-haired one." Form of Lloyd. Floyd McKissick, civil rights activist; Floyd Patterson, boxer.

Flynn (Irish Gaelic) "Son of the red-haired one." **Flin, Flinn**

Forbes (Irish Gaelic) "Owner of the fields." A Scottish clan name.

Ford (Old English) "Shallow part of the river where crossing is easy." Ford Maddox Ford, British novelist.

Forrest (Old French) "Forest or woodsman." **Forest, Forester, Forrester, Forrie, Forster, Foss, Foster**

Francis (Latin) "One who is from France." St. Francis of Assisi; Sir Francis Bacon, painter; Franco Corelli, opera singer; Francis Ford Coppola, movie director; François Mitterrand, French president; Franco Zeffirelli, stage designer and director. **Franc, Francesco, Francisco, Franco, François, Frans, Frants**

Franklin (Middle English) "Free man," referring to a free landholder who is not of noble birth. Franklin Pierce, Franklin D. Roosevelt, fourteenth and thirty-second U.S. presidents, respectively; Frankie Avalon, actor; Franz Kline, U.S. painter; Frank Perdue, entrepreneur; Frank Lloyd Wright, architect; Frank Zappa, rock musician. **Frank, Frankie, Franklyn, Franz**

Frazer (Old English) "Curly-haired one." (French) "With strawberry coloring." **Fraser, Frasier, Frazier**

Fredrick (Old German) "Peaceful ruler." Frederick the Great, Prussian king; Federico Fellini, film director. **Eric, Federico, Fred, Frederic, Fredric, Fredrik, Friedrich, Fritz, Fryderyk, Rick**

Freeman (Old English) "A man who is free." **Freedham**

Fremont (Old German) "One who guards freedom." **Free, Monty**

Fuller (Middle English) "One who works with cloth."

Fulton (Old English) "From the field full of fowl." **Fult**

Boys
G

Gabel (Old French) "A small Gabriel." **Gabe, Gable**

Gabriel (Hebrew) Biblical name meaning "my strength is in God." Gabriel was the archangel of the Annunciation. **Gabby, Gabe, Gabi, Gabor, Gaby**

Gage (Old French) "One who gives his pledge."

Gair (Irish Gaelic) "Small one."

Gaius (Latin) "One who rejoices." **Cai, Caio, Caius**

Galen (Greek) "Small, calm, healer." **Gael, Gaelen, Gale, Gayle**

Gallagher (Irish Gaelic) "One who is eager to help."

Gardner (Middle English) "A gardner." Gardner Cowles, publisher of *Look* magazine. **Gard, Gardener, Gardiner**

Garfield (Old English) "From the battlefield." **Field, Gar**

Garner (Old English) "A warrior who shelters and protects." **Garnet, Garnett**

Garrett (Old English) "Mighty warrior." (Welsh) "Gentle one." Form of Gerard. Garrett Hobart, twenty-fourth U.S. vice president. **Garret, Garrot, Garrott, Jarret, Jarrett**

Garrick (Old English) "One who rules with a spear." **Garek, Garik, Garrek, Rick**

Garrison (Old English) "Son of Garrett." Garrison Keillor, radio personality.

Garson (Old English) "Son of the man with a spear." Garson Kanin, playwright. **Gars, Garsy**

Garth (Scandinavian) "One who cares for the garden." Garth Brooks, country music singer. **Gar, Gareth**

Garvey (Irish Gaelic) "One who has battled for peace." **Garvy**

Gary (Old English) "Man with a spear." Gary Cooper, actor; Garry Trudeau, U.S. cartoonist. **Garry**

Gaston (Old French) "From the town of Gascony." Villainous character in the Walt Disney movie *Beauty and the Beast*.

Gavin (Welsh) "Like a white hawk or falcon." Gavin McLeod, actor. **Gavan, Gaven, Gawain**

Gaylord (Old French) "One with high spirits." Gaylord Perry, baseball pitcher. **Gailard, Gayelord, Gaylor**

Gaynor (Welsh) "Blessed son of the white-haired man." **Gainer, Gaines, Gainor, Gayner**

Geiger (German) "One who plays the violin."

Gene (Greek) "Well-born one." Short form of Eugene. Gene Hackman, actor; Gene Kelly, dancer; Gene Shalit, broadcast journalist and critic.

Geoffrey (Old German) "One with the peace of God." Form of Godfrey and Jeffrey. **Geoff, Geoffredo, Geoffry, Gofredo, Geofrey, Gottfrid, Gottfried, Jeffrey**

George (Greek) "Farmer; one who works the land." The name of many English kings. George Washington and George Bush, first and forty-first U.S. presidents, respectively; George Gershwin, composer; George Lucas, movie director and producer; George C. Scott, actor; George Bernard Shaw, playwright. **Georges, Georgie, Georgy, Giorgio, Goran, Jorge, Yurik**

Gerald (Old German) "Spear warrior or ruler." Gerard Depardieu, French actor; Gerald Ford, thirty-eighth U.S. president; Geraldo Rivera, TV talk show host. **Geraldo, Gerard, Geraud, Gerhard, Gerhardt, Gerry, Giraud, Jerrold, Jerry**

Germain (Latin) "Brotherly one." (Middle English) "A little sprout." **Germaine, Jermain, Jermaine**

Gershom (Hebrew) Biblical name meaning "a sojourner" or "a stranger." Gershom is a son of Moses.

Gervaise (Old German) "Honorable warrior." **Gervais, Gervas, Gervasi, Gervasio**

Gideon (Hebrew) Biblical name meaning "one who cuts down trees." **Gedeon, Gideone, Gidon**

Gifford (Old English) "A brave giver" or "one with chubby little cheeks." **Giffard, Gifferd**

Gilbert (Old English) "Trusted one." **Bert, Burt, Gib, Gilberto, Gill, Guilbert, Wilbert, Wilbur, Will**

Giles (Latin) "One who carries a shield." (Greek) "Youthful, lightly bearded one." **Gelles, Gide, Gil, Gill, Gilles, Gyles**

Gillespie (Scottish Gaelic) "A servant to the bishop."

Gillette (Old French) "Small, trusted one." **Gelette, Gillett**

Gilroy (Irish Gaelic) "Son of the red-haired one." **Gildero, Gildroy, Gill, Gilly**

Giovanni (Italian) "God is gracious." Form of John. **Gianni, Vanni**

Giuseppe (Italian) "God shall add." Giuseppe Verdi, Italian composer. **Giuseppi, Seppi**

Glen (Irish Gaelic) "From the valley or glen." Glen Campbell, country entertainer; Glenn Miller, bandleader. **Glenn, Glyn, Glynn**

Goddard (Old English) "One who believes in God's strength." **Godard, Gotthard, Gotthart**

Godfrey (Old German) "One who has the peace of God." **Godfried, Gottfried**

Godwin (Old English) "A friend of God." **Godewyn, Goodwin, Win, Winnie**

Golding (Old English) "From the golden one."

Gomer (Hebrew) Biblical name meaning "one who is famous in battle." Gomer is the son of Jepheth and grandson of Noah. Gomer Pyle, TV character on *The Andy Griffith Show.*

Gordon (Scottish Gaelic) "A hero." (Old English) "One who lives on a wedge-shaped hill." A Scottish clan name. Gordon Lightfoot, singer and songwriter; Gore Vidal, American writer. **Gordan, Gorden, Gordie, Gordy, Gore**

Grady (Irish Gaelic) "Illustrious one." **Gradey**

Graham (Old English) "From the gravel-covered estate." Graham Greene, writer; Graham Nash, rock musician. **Graehme, Graeme, Grahame, Gram**

Grant (French) "Great or large one." Grant Wood, painter. **Grantland, Grantley, Granville, Grenville**

Gregory (Greek) "A watchman." The name of sixteen popes. Gregory Hines and Gregory Peck, actors; Greg Allman, rock musician. **Graig, Greer, Greg, Gregers, Gregg, Gregor, Greig, Goito**

Grey (Old English) "From the grey-haired man." (Middle English) "A bailiff." **Gray, Grayson, Greyson**

Griffith (Welsh) "One who is strong in faith." **Griff, Griffin**

Griswold (Old German) "From the gray forest." **Gris, Griz**

Grover (Old English) "From the grove." Grover Cleveland, twenty-second and twenty-fourth U.S. president. **Grove**

Gunther (Old German) "Warrior." Günter Grass, German writer; Gunner Myrdal, Swedish social scientist. **Gunnar, Gunner, Gunter**

Gustav (Swedish) "One who carries God's staff." Gustave

Flaubert, author of *Madame Bovary;* Gustav Klimt, Austrian painter. **Gustaf, Gustaff, Gustave**

Guthrie (Irish Gaelic) "From the place where the wind blows." (Old German) "Noble warrior." **Guthrey**

Guy (Old German) "Warrior." Guy Fawkes, English conspirator; Guy Lombardo, bandleader. **Guido**

BOYS
H

Haag (Dutch) "A keeper of the hedges or fences." **Haig**

Hadley (Old English) "From the heath-covered valley." **Haddon, Haden, Hadlee, Hadleigh, Hadyn**

Haldan (Scandinavian) "Half Danish," referring to a man half Danish and half English. Hal Linden, actor. **Dan, Hal, Halden**

Hakeem (Arabic) "Wise." **Hakim**

Hall (Old English) "From the hall or manor." **Hale, Halford, Halstead, Halsted, Heall**

Halsey (Old English) "From Hal's Island." **Halsie**

Halston (Scandinavian) "Sturdy and invincible like a rock." **Hallstein**

Hamilton (Old English) "From the hamlet on the mountain." Hamlet, famous Shakespearean character. **Ham, Hamil, Hamlet, Tony**

Hamlin (Old English) "One who loves and rules his home or hamlet." **Ham, Hamlen, Lin, Lynn**

Hanley (Old English) "From the high meadow." **Hanlee, Hanleigh, Hanlie**

Hans (Scandinavian) Form of John. Hans Christian Andersen, writer. Hans Hofmann, artist. **Hannes, Hansi, Hanus**

Harcourt (Old French) "From the fortress." **Harry, Court**

Hardan (Old English) "From the land full of hares." (Old German) "From the army land." **Harden, Hardin**

Harding (Old English) "Hardy and brave."

Hardy (Old German) "Bold and strong." **Hardey, Hardie, Harding**

Hargrove (Old English) "From the grove of hares." **Hargrave, Hargreaves**

Harley (Old English) "From the woods full of hares." (Old German) "Warrior." **Arley, Harlan, Harland, Harlen, Harlin**

Harlow (Old English) "From the hill with the army camp." **Arlo**

Harold (Old English) "Ruler of the army." The name of two kings of England and three kings of Norway. Harold Pinter, British playwright. **Harald, Harry, Herald, Herold**

Harper (Old English) "One who plays the harp." Harper Lee, American writer; Harpo Marx, comedian. **Harp, Harpo, Harpor**

Harrison (Old English) "Son of Harry." Harrison Ford, actor. **Harris**

Harry (Old English) "Lord or ruler of the home." A form of Harold or Henry. Harry Belafonte, Harry Chapin, Harry Connick, Jr., singers; Harry S. Truman, thirty-third U.S. president.

Hartley (Old English) "From the meadow with deer." Hart Crane, American poet. **Hart**

Hartwell (Old English) "From near the spring where deer drink."

Harvey (Celtic) "One who is able in battle." Harve Bernard, fashion designer. **Harv, Herve**

Hasan (Arabic) "One who is good." **Husayn, Husni, Ihsan**

Haskel (Hebrew) "One who is understanding or wise." **Ezekiel, Haskell**

Haslett (Old English) "From the hazel tree land." **Hazlett**

Hass (Old German) "Harelike."

Hassan (Arabic) "Handsome one." **Hasen, Hassin**

Hastings (Old English) "Son of the violent one." **Hastie, Hasty**

Haven (Old English) "From the safe place."

Hawthorne (Old English) "One who lives near a hawthorn tree." **Hawthorn**

Hayden (Old English) "From the valley of hedges." **Hadyn, Haydon, Hayes**

Hayward (Old English) "Guardian of the hedged wood." **Hays, Heywood, Wood, Woodie, Woody**

Heath (Middle English) "From the heath-covered lands." Heathcliff, protagonist in *Wuthering Heights* by Emily Brontë. **Heathcliff**

Hector (Greek) "Steadfast, firm." In Greek mythology, Hector is one of the bravest Trojan warriors. **Etor, Ettore, Hechtor, Heck**

Helmut (Old German) "Courageous warrior." Helmut Kohl, chancellor of Germany. **Helmuth**

Henderson (Old English) "Son of Henry." **Hendi, Hendie**

Henry (Old German) "Ruler of the home or estate." Hank Aaron, baseball player; Henry Fonda, actor; Henry Ford, automobile engineer; Henry James, writer; Henry Kissinger, U.S. secretary of state; Henri Matisse, French painter. **Enrico, Enrique, Hal, Hank, Harry, Heinrich, Hendrick, Henrik, Henri**

Herbert (Old German) "Brilliant warrior." Herb Albert, bandleader; Herbert Hoover, thirty-first U.S. president. **Bert, Herb, Herbie**

Hercules (Greek) "God's glory." Strongest man in Greek mythology. **Hercule, Herculie**

Herman (Old German) "An army man." Herman Kahn, physicist and futurologist; Herman Melville, author of *Moby Dick;* Herman Wouk, novelist. **Armand, Armin, Harman, Harmon, Hermann, Hermie, Hermon, Hermy**

Herschel (Hebrew) "Deerlike." **Hersch, Hersh, Hershel, Hershi, Hirsch, Hirsh**

Hilary (Latin) "Cheerful." **Hill, Hillary, Hillery**

Hillel (Hebrew) "Praised one."

Hilton (Old English) "From the town on the hill." **Hylton**

Hiram (Hebrew) Biblical name meaning "of noble birth." Hiram is the biblical king of Tyre. **Hi, Hirom, Hurom, Hy, Hyrum**

Hobart (Old German) "Highly brilliant one." **Hobard, Hobie, Hobey**

Hodding (Dutch) "Bricklayer."

Hogan (Irish Gaelic) "Youthful one." **Hogie**

Holbrook (Old English) "From the brook in the hollows." **Brooke, Holbrooke.**

Holden (Old English) "From the deep or hollow valley." Holden Caufield, main character in *The Catcher in the Rye.* **Holcomb, Holcombe**

Holger (Scandinavian) "From the island of warriors." **Hogge**

Hollis (Old English) "From the grove of the holly trees." **Holly**

Holmes (Middle English) "From the river islands."

Holt (Old English) "From near the woods."

Homer (Greek) "Of a pledge." Name of the author of *The Iliad* and *The Odyssey*. **Homere, Omero**

Honore (Latin) "Honored one." Honoré de Balzac, French novelist. **Honor, Honoratus, Honorius, Honnor**

Horace (Latin) "A keeper of time." Roman clan name. Horace Mann, educator; Horatio Alger, novelist. **Horacio, Horatio, Horatius, Orry**

Horst (Old German) "From the wooded hill." (Old English) "Stallionlike."

Horton (Old English) "From the muddy estate." **Horten, Orton**

Houston (Old English) "From the hill town." (Scottish) "Of Hugh's town."

Howard (Old English) "Guardian or watchman." Howard Cosell, TV sportscaster; Howard Hughes, American businessman. **Howey, Howie, Ward**

Howell (Old English) "From the hill." (Old German) "Eminent one." **Howe, Howel**

Hoyt (Middle English) "Small boat." **Hoyle, Hoit**

Hubert (Old German) "Of bright mind and spirit." Hubert Humphrey, American politician and thirty-eighth U.S. vice president. **Hobart, Hube, Huberto, Hubie, Huburt, Humberto, Uberto**

Hudson (Old English) "Son of the one with a hood" or "son of Hyde."

Hugh (Old English) "Intelligent, spirited one." Hugh Hefner, magazine publisher; Huey Newton, political activist. **Hewett, Hewitt, Huck, Huey, Hughes, Hugo, Huw, Ugo**

Hume (Scandinavian) "From the grassy hill." Hume Cronyn, actor and director.

Humphrey (Old German) "Young warrior of peace." Humphrey Bogart, actor. **Humfry, Humfrey, Hump, Humph, Humphry**

Hunter (Old English) "A hunter." Hunter Thompson, journalist. **Hunt**

Huntington (Old English) "From the hunter's town on the hill." **Hunt, Huntingdon**

Huntley (Old English) "From the hunter's meadow." **Hunt, Huntlee, Huntleigh, Huntly, Lee, Leigh**

Hurst (Middle English) "From the forest." **Hearst**

Hussein (Arabic) "Little, handsome one." Decandant of the Prophet Muhammad. **Husain, Husein**

Hyatt (Old English) "From the high gate." **Hy**

Hyde (Old English) "From the hide," a unit of land measuring 120 acres.

Hyman (English) "Of life." Form of Chaim. **Hy, Hymie, Mannie**

BOYS
I

Iago (Spanish) (Welsh) Form of James. Name of the famous villain in Shakespeare's *Othello*.

Ian (Scottish Gaelic) "Gracious one." Form of John. Ian Fleming, writer. **Iain**

Ichabod (Hebrew) Biblical name meaning "where is his glory?" Ichabod Crane, character in Washington Irving's *The Legend of Sleepy Hollow*.

Ignatius (Latin) "Fiery one." St. Ignatius, first-century saint. **Iggy, Ignace, Ignacio, Ignacius, Ignazio, Inigo, Nacek, Nacho**

Igor (Scandinavian) "An army hero." Igor Stravinsky, composer. **Ivor**

Ilie (Romanian) Form of Elias. Ilie Nastase, tennis player.

Ingemar (Scandinavian) "Famous son." Ingmar Bergman, filmmaker. **Ingar, Inger, Ingmar**

Innes (Irish Gaelic) "From the islands." **Inness, Innis**

Ira (Hebrew) Biblical name meaning "watchful one." Ira Gershwin, lyricist.

Irving (Irish Gaelic) "Handsome one." (Old English) "Sea-lover." Irving Berlin, composer; Irving Stone, writer. **Earvin, Ervin, Erwin, Irv, Irvin, Irvine, Irwin**

Isaac (Hebrew) Biblical name meaning "one who laughs." Son of Abraham and Sarah. Isaac Asimov, writer; Sir Isaac Newton, mathematician. **Eise, Ike, Isaak, Isac, Isak, Izaak**

Isaiah (Hebrew) Biblical name meaning "God is my salvation." Name of the great Hebrew prophet. **Isa, Isaia, Isiah, Issiah**

Ishmael (Hebrew) "God hears." A character in Herman Melville's *Moby Dick*.

Isidore (Greek) "A gift." Name held by many saints. **Dore, Dorian, Dory, Isador, Isadore, Issy, Izzy**

Israel (Hebrew) Biblical name meaning "one who wrestles with the Lord," which is literally what Jacob did, and because of his strength, God gave him the name Israel. The name has taken on a new meaning, "the Jewish nation," with the founding of the State of Israel in 1948. Israel J. Singer, novelist and brother of Isaac Bashevis Singer. **Iser, Issur, Sroel**

Italo (Latin) "One from Italy." In Roman mythology, Italus is the father of Romulus and Remus, founders of Rome. Italo Calvino, Italian writer. **Itala, Italia, Italus**

Itamar (Hebrew) Biblical name meaning "one from the island of palms."

Ivan (Russian) "God is gracious." Ivan Lendl, tennis player; Ivan Pavlov, Russian physiologist. Form of John. **Ion, Ivor, Iwan**

BOYS
J

Jabez (Hebrew) Biblical name meaning "one who causes pain," referring to the pain of childbirth. **Jabe, Jabes, Jabus**

Jabir (Arabic) "One who comforts and restores." **Jabr, Gabir, Gabr**

Jackson (English) "Son of Jack." A form of John or Jacob. Jackson Brown, pop singer; Jackson Pollock, artist. **Jack, Jackie, Jacky**

Jacob (Hebrew) Biblical name meaning "One who trips up another, a supplanter." Jacob was the son of Abraham who "supplanted" his slightly older twin brother, Esau. Jackie Gleason, comedian; Jack Nicholson, actor; Jack Nicklaus, golfer. **Cob, Cobb, Cobus, Hamish, Jack, Jackie, Jacques, Jaime, Jake, Jakob, James, Jamie, Jay, Jim, Seamus, Shamus, Yakov**

Jamal (Arabic) "Handsome one." **Jamaal, Jamahl, Jamel, Jamell, Jamil**

James (Middle English) Form of Jacob. The name became popular when James Stuart took over the throne of England in 1603. James Buchanan, fifteenth U.S. president; Jacques Cousteau, French marine explorer; Jimmy Dorsey, bandleader; Jimi Hendrix and James Taylor, rock musicians; James Earl Jones and James Stewart, actors; James Michener, writer; Giacamo Puccini, Italian composer. **Giacamo, Giacomo, Hamish, Iago, Jacques, Jago, Jaime, Jamie, Jay, Jem, Jim, Jimi, Jimmy, Seamus, Shamus**

Jared (Hebrew) Biblical name meaning "a descendant or inheritor." Jared was a descendant of Adam. **Jarod, Jarred, Jarrett, Jarrod, Jerd, Yered**

Jarek (Slavic) "One born in January." **Januisz, Janus, Jaromil, Jaromir, Jaruse**

Jarvis (Old German) "Proficient with a spear." Form of Gervais. **Gervis, Jervis**

Jason (Greek) "Healer." Jason Robards, Jr., actor. In classical mythology it is Jason who searches for the Golden Fleece. **Jase, Jasen, Jay, Jayson**

Jasper (Persian) "Master of treasure." A form of Gaspar, which is the name of one of the three wise men who bring gifts to the baby Jesus. Jasper Johns, artist. **Gaspare, Jesper, Kaspar**

Jay (Old French) "One who chatters like the jaybird." **Jayme, Jeay, Jeye**

Jedidiah (Hebrew) Biblical name meaning "friend of the Lord." **Jed, Jedediah**

Jefferson (Old English) "Son of Jeffrey." Jefferson Davis, Confederate president. **Jeff**

Jeffrey (English) "One with the peace of God." Form of Geoffrey. Jeff Bridges, actor. **Jefery, Jeff, Jefferey, Jeffie, Jeffrie, Jeffry**

Jeremiah (Hebrew) Biblical name meaning "God's appointed one." Jeremiah was the renowned prophet of Judah. Jeremy Irons, actor. **Jem, Jeramey, Jeramie, Jere, Jereme, Jeremias, Jeremie, Jeremy, Jeromy, Jerry**

Jerome (Latin) "Sacred named one." Jerry Garcia, rock musician; Jerome Robbins, dancer and choreographer. **Geronimo, Gerry, Jeronimo, Jerry**

Jerzy (Polish) "One who works the land." Jerzy Kosinski, American writer. **Jurek**

Jesse (Hebrew) Biblical name meaning "God's gift" or "of the grace of God." Jesse is the father of King David and ultimately from whom Jesus is descended. Jesse Jackson, political leader; Jesse Owens, track and field athlete. **Jess**

Jethro (Hebrew) Biblical name meaning "preeminent one." Jethro is the father-in-law of Moses. Jethro Tull, agricultural reformer (1674). **Jeth**

Joab (Hebrew) "One who praises the Lord."

Joachim (Hebrew) Biblical name meaning "established by God." Joachim is one of the names ascribed to the father of the Virgin Mary. **Achim, Akim, Joaquim, Jochen, Jochim, Jockum, Yakim**

Job (Hebrew) Biblical name meaning "persecuted." This is the name held by the hero of the Book of Job, a uniquely patient and faithful man who endures severe maltreatment imposed by God. Thus the saying "He has the patience of Job." **Jobe, Jobst**

Joel (Hebrew) Biblical name meaning "God is the Lord." Joel Grey, actor.

John (Hebrew) Biblical name meaning "God's gracious gift." Common Christian name after John the Baptist, John the Apostle, and John the Evangelist. Johann Sebastian Bach, composer; John Belushi, comedian; Johnny Carson, TV personality; John Cheever, American writer; Jean Piaget, Swiss psychologist. **Evan, Ewan, Ewen, Giovanni, Hans, Iain, Ian, Jack, Jackie, Jan, Jean, Jock, Jocko, Johan, Johann, Johannes, Johnnie, Johnny, Jon, Juan, Owen, Sean, Shaughn, Shawn, Yannick, Zane**

Jonah (Hebrew) Biblical name meaning "dove." Jonah is the prophet who was thrown overboard and swallowed by a whale. **Ionas, Jonas**

Jonathan (Hebrew) Biblical name meaning "God has given." Jonathan is a true friend to the biblical King David. Jon Voight, actor. **Jon, Jonathan, Jonathon**

Jordan (Hebrew) "One who descends" or "flows downward," referring to the waters of the Jordan River, where Christ was baptized. Judd Hirsh, actor. **Giordano, Jared, Jerad, Joord, Jordon, Jori, Jory, Jourdain, Judd**

José Spanish form of Joseph. José Ferrer, actor, director, and producer. **Pepe, Pepito**

Joseph (Hebrew) Biblical name meaning "God shall add," referring to the giving of additional children. In the Old Testament, Joseph is the favorite son of Jacob. In the New Testament, Joseph is the husband of the Virgin Mary. Joey Bishop, comedian; Joseph Conrad, English writer; Joe DiMaggio, baseball player. **Che, Giuseppe, Jo, Joe, Joey, Jose, Josef, Josep, Yosef**

Joshua (Hebrew) Biblical name meaning "one whose salvation is God." After the death of Moses, Joshua led the Israelites into the promised land. **Josh, Joshia, Joshuah, Josua, Yehosha**

Josiah (Hebrew) Biblical name meaning "one who God heals or protects." Biblical king of Judah. Josiah Wedgwood, English potter and founder of Wedgwood china. **Josh, Josias**

Judah (Hebrew) Biblical name meaning "praised one." Judas Iscariot is the biblical apostle who betrayed Christ. Name of the protagonist in Thomas Hardy's *Jude the Obscure*. **Juda, Judas, Judd, Jude**

Julian (Latin) "Youthful one." Julius Caesar, Roman emperor; Jules Feiffer, cartoonist; Julio Iglesias and Julien

Lennon, singers; Julius Erving (Dr. J), basketball player.
Jule, Jules, Julien, Julio, Julius
Justin (Latin) "One who is fair or just." **Justen, Justino, Justinus, Justis, Justus, Justyn**

■ How Many Names Is The Right Number? ■

There is no law stating how many names a person need have. Obviously Adam and Eve didn't have a last, much less a middle name. As the population grew, so did the need to distinguish one person from another. Imagine, for example, that in the village by the broad river crossing there is a John, and another John arrives. Suddenly it is necessary to differentiate one John from the other. Let's say the new John has red hair. He then becomes John Reid or John Russell. And the John who lives by the broad river crossing (or ford) becomes John Bradford.

Today the accepted number of names seems to be three. The need for four names will surely arise. However, remember the problem Diana Spencer had saying the full name of her husband (Charles Philip Arthur George Windsor) during their wedding ceremony? Does anyone really need that many names?

BOYS
K

Kai (Scandinavian) "Chickenlike." (Hawaiian) "From the sea." Kai Siegbahn, Nobel Prize-winning physicist. **Kaj, Ky, Kye**

Kalil (Arabic) "Good friend." Kahlil Gibran, writer. **Kahaleel, Kahill, Kahlil, Kailil, Khalil**

Kane (Irish Gaelic) "Tribute." **Kain, Kaine, Kayne**

Kareem (Arabic) "Of noble birth." Kareem Abdul-Jabbar, basketball player. **Karam, Karim**

Karl (German) "Manly one." Form of Charles. The name of seven Austrian emperors. **Carl, Kalle, Karlan, Karlens, Karlis**

Karp (Greek) "Fruitful or productive one." **Carpus, Karpos, Karpus**

Kaufman (German) "A merchant or tradesman."

Keane (Old English) "Sharp or keen one." (Irish Gaelic) "Ancient." **Cian, Kean, Keen, Keenan, Keene, Keeney, Kienan**

Keegen (Irish Gaelic) "Little, fiery one." **Egan**

Keenan (Irish Gaelic) "Small, ancient one." (Old English) "Wise one." **Keanan, Keeney, Kienan**

Kees (Dutch) "A leader" or "carrier of the war horn." **Cees**

Keifer (Irish Gaelic) "Handsome, gentle one." Kiefer Sutherland, actor. **Keefe, Keeffe, Kiefer**

Keir (Scottish) "Dark-skinned." **Kerr**

Keith (Scottish Gaelic) "From the woods." Keith Carradine, singer and actor; Keith Haring, artist; Keith Richards, rock musician.

Kelan (Irish Gaelic) "Slender one." **Keelan**

Kelly (Irish Gaelic) "A warrior." **Keller, Kelley**

Kelvin (Irish Gaelic) "From the river." Calvin Klein, fashion designer. **Calvin, Kalvyn, Kelwin**

Kemp (Old English) "Warrior." (Middle English) "Athlete or wrestler." **Kempe**

Kendall (Welsh) "From the clear river valley." **Ken, Kendell**

Kendrick (Welsh) "From the high hill." Possibly a contraction of MacKenrick or MacEanraig, meaning "son of Henry." **Ken, Kendricks, Kenrick, Rick**

Kenelm (Old English) "Brave, helmeted one."

Kennard (Old English) "Strong, brave guardian." **Kenard**

Kennedy (Irish Gaelic) "One with a misshapen or helmeted head." An old Scottish and Irish clan name. Today, a name given to honor President John F. Kennedy.

Kenneth (Irish Gaelic) "Handsome, fiery one." Kenneth Grahame, author of *Wind in the Willows;* Kenny Loggins and Kenny Rodgers, singers. **Ken, Kennett, Kennith, Kenny**

Kent (Welsh) "From the border" or "bright white one." **Kennet**

Kenton (Old English) "From the ruler's estate."

Kenyon (Irish Gaelic) "Blond-haired one." **Kennie, Kenny**

Kermit (Irish Gaelic) "One who is free." **Ker, Kermie, Kermy**

Kerry (Irish Gaelic) "Dark-haired one." **Keary, Kerr**

Kerwin (Irish Gaelic) "One with a dark complexion." **Kerwaine, Kerwinn**

Kevin (Irish Gaelic) "Kind, handsome one." Kevin Costner and Kevin Kline, actors. **Kev, Kevan, Kevyn**

Kieran (Irish Gaelic) "Dark black one." The name of fifteen Irish saints. **Kearen, Kearon, Kyran**

Killian (Irish Gaelic) "Small, warlike one." **Cillian, Kilian**

Kiley (Irish Gaelic) "Handsome, graceful one." **Kiel, Kile, Kyle, Kylie, Kyley**

Kimball (Old English) "A royal chief" or "from the royal hill." Kimball O'Hara is the hero in Rudyard Kipling's novel *Jungle Book*. **Kim**

King (Old English) "A ruler." A name used to commemorate Dr. Martin Luther King, Jr.

Kingsley (Old English) "From the King's woods." Kingsley Amis, English novelist. **King, Kingsly, Kingsten, Kingston, Kinsley**

Kipp (Old English) "From the peak of the hill." **Kip, Kipper, Kippie, Kippy**

Kirby (Old English) "From the town with a church." **Kerby**

Kirk (Scandinavian) "From the church." Kirk Cameron and Kirk Douglas, actors. **Kerk, Kirke, Kirkley**

Klaus (German) "One of the victorious people." Form of Nikolaus. **Claus, Klaas, Klaes**

Knight (Middle English) "A knight or soldier."

Knox (Old English) "From the hill." **Knocks**

Knut (Scandinavian) "Knotlike." **Canute, Cnut, Knud, Knute**

Kohler (German) "One who burns charcoal."

Kolbert (German) "Short-haired one." **Kolb, Kolbe, Kohlhardt**

Konrad (German) "Brave, wise counselor." Form of Conrad. **Kondrat, Kondrati**

Krishna (Hindi) "Delightful one." **Krisha**

Kristian (Danish) "Christian one." Form of Christian.

Kristopher (Scandinavian) Form of Christopher. Kris Kristofferson, singer and actor. **Kris, Kristofer**

Kurt (German) Form of Conrad or Curtis. Kurt Vonnegut, Jr., writer; Kurt Waldheim, Austrian president and diplomat.

Boys
L

Laban (Hebrew) "White one."

Lachlan (Scottish Gaelic) "From Norway," referring to the "land of the lochs." **Lach, Lache, Lachie, Laughlin, Lockie**

Ladd (Middle English) "An attendant." **Lad, Ladde**

Ladislo (Italian) "A famous leader." **Ladislas, Ladislav, Ladislow, Laszlo**

Laird (Scottish) "One who owns land."

Lamar (Old German) "Well known throughout the land." **Lamarr, Lemar**

Lambert (Old German) "Bright and famous throughout the land." **Bert, Lamberto, Lammert, Lanbert**

Lamont (Scandinavian) "A lawyer." **Lammont, Lamond, Monty**

Lance (Old German) "From the land." (Latin). "One who serves another." Sir Lancelot, infamous character in the legends of King Arthur. **Lancelot, Lanzo, Launce, Launcelot**

Landon (Old English) "Of the open land." **Landan, Lander**

Lane (Middle English) "Of the road or lane." **Layne**

Lang (Scandinavian) "Tall or long one."

Langdon (Old English) "Of the long, open hill." **Landon, Langsdon, Langston**

Langford (Old English) "Of the long ford."

Langley (Old English) "Of the long valley." **Lang, Langly**

Langston (Old English) "Of the long village or town." Langston Hughes, American poet. **Langsworth**

Lars (Scandinavian) Form of Lawrence. **Larson**

Latham (Scandinavian) "One who works or lives in the barn." **Laith, Lathe**

■ JUNIOR!!!! ■

This charming sobriquet—often bestowed with the best intentions—may become an unfortunate nickname for every boy with the misfortune to be named after his father.

A call for "Frank" will summon both father and son—and in some families, grandson—to a ringing telephone. But these infrequent annoyances are hardly sufficient grounds for abandoning the notion of naming your son after his dad, especially if there is a tradition in your family of passing names from one generation to the next. A name thus bequeathed can be a source of pride for both parties.

However, bear in mind these few provisos:

You can avoid confusion by passing along your first and last names and choosing a unique middle name for your child. Simply call him by his middle name. But don't be disappointed when he comes home from the first day of school to tell you that he had your name all along "and didn't even know it."

If you choose the "Junior" route, whatever your intention, your son will probably one day feel that he has been called upon to fill a big pair of shoes.

Be prepared to hear your proud name transformed into a playground nickname that is clearly not of your choosing. If the mere idea of that makes you wince, consider giving your son a nickname before he is given one by his playmates.

That being said, here are some famous Juniors who have made a name for themselves, just in case you need a little encouragement:

Harry Connick, Jr.
John Glenn, Jr.
Berry Gordy, Jr.
Douglas Fairbanks, Jr.
Martin Luther King, Jr.
Oliver Wendell Holmes, Jr.
Adam Clayton Powell, Jr.
Jason Robards, Jr.
Kurt Vonnegut, Jr.

Lathrop (Old English) "From the village with a barn."
Lathe, Lathrope, Thrope

Latimer (Middle English) "One who interprets Latin." **Lattie**

Laurence, Lawrence (Latin) "One who wears a crown
of laurels." Sir Laurence Olivier, English actor; Larry
Bird, basketball player **Larry, Lars, Laurens, Laurent,
Lawrance, Lawrie, Lawry, Lawson, Lon, Lonnie, Loren-
cio, Lorenz, Lorenzo, Lorin, Lorne, Lorry**

Lawford (Old English) "One who lives near the ford in the
hill." **Ford, Fordy, Law, Lawson**

Lazarus (Hebrew) Biblical name meaning "God is my helper."
In the New Testament, Lazarus was raised from the dead by
Jesus. **Eleazar, Laz, Lazar, Lazare, Lazaros**

Leander (Greek) "One who is courageous like a lion."
Ander, Leandre, Leandro

Lee (Old English) "One who comes from the meadow or
clearing." An English place name used as both a first and a
last name. Lee Iacocca, U.S. businessman; Lee Majors,
actor; Lee Harvey Oswald, assassin; Lee Strasberg, actor,
director, and teacher. **Leigh**

Leib (Hebrew) "Lionlike." **Lavi, Leibel**

Leif (Scandinavian) "A beloved heir." Leif Ericsson, explorer. **Leiv, Lief**

Leighton (Old English) "From the settlement in the meadow."
Layton, Leigh

Leland (Old English) "From the open land." Leland Hayward, movie producer. **Leeland, Liland**

Lemuel (Hebrew) Biblical name meaning "one devoted to
God." Name of the hero in Jonathan Swift's *Gulliver's
Travels*. **Lem, Lemmie, Lemmy**

Leo (Latin) "Lion." Astrological sign for those born between
July 22 and August 23. Leo Tolstoy, Russian writer; Leon
Trotsky, Russian political leader; Leon Uris, author. **Leon,
Lev, Lyon**

Leonard (Old German) "One as strong and brave as a lion."
Leonard Bernstein, conductor and composer; Leonard Skin-
ner, rock singer. **Len, Lenard, Lennie, Lenny, Leonardo,
Leonerd**

Leopold (Old German) "Patriotic protector." Leopold I, II,
and III, kings of Belgium. **Leopoldo, Luitpold, Poldi**

Leroy (Old French) "A king or ruler." **Elroy, Roy**

Lester (Old English) "From the town of Leicester." Lester
Lanin, orchestra conductor. **Leicester, Les**

Levi (Hebrew) Biblical name meaning "joined or attached."

Third son of Jacob and Leah. So named because of Leah's hope that by giving Jacob three sons, this would keep them forever joined. **Lev, Levey, Levin, Levy, Lewi**

Lewis, Louis (Old German) "Famous, heroic warrior." The name of many French kings, including Louis I, the son of Charlemagne, and Louis XIV, "the Sun King." Louis Armstrong, jazz musician; Lewis Carroll, author of *Alice in Wonderland;* Luigi Pirandello, Italian writer. **Clovis, Lew, Lewey, Lou, Louie, Ludvig, Ludvik, Ludwig, Luigi, Luis**

Liam (Irish) Form of William. Liam O'Flaherty, Irish writer. **Uilliam**

Lincoln (Old English) "Of the colony near the lake." Name used to commemorate Abraham Lincoln, sixteenth U.S. president. **Linc, Link**

Lindberg (Old German) "From the hill of linden trees." **Linberg, Lindell, Lindly, Lindy, Lynberg**

Linus (Greek) "Fair-haired one." A character from the Charles Schulz's *Peanuts* comic strip who carries a security blanket. Dr. Linus Pauling, winner of two Nobel prizes.

Lionel (Old French) "Like a lion cub." Lionel Richie, pop singer. **Lionello, Lyonel**

Lisle (Latin) "From the isle or island." **Lyall, Lyell, Lyle**

Litton (Old English) "From the town on the hill." Lytton Strachey, English writer. **Lytton**

Livingstone (Old English) "From Leif's estate."

Llewellyn (Welsh) "Bold and fast as a lion." The name of many Welsh royals, including the thirteenth-century ruler Llewellyn the Great. **Lew, Lewis, Llywellyn, Wells**

Lloyd (Welsh) "Gray-haired one." Lloyd Bridges, actor. **Floyd, Loyd, Loyde**

Locke (Old English) "From the settlement in the woods." **Lock, Lockland**

Logan (Scottish Gaelic) "From the lowland or hollow." A Scottish clan name.

Loman (Irish Gaelic) "Enlightened one."

Lombard (Latin) "One with a long beard." **Lombardi, Lombardo**

Lorcan (Irish Gaelic) "Fierce one." **Lorke**

Lorimer (Middle English) "A harness- or saddlemaker." **Lorrimer**

Lorne (English) Form of Lawrence. Lorne Greene, Lorne Michaels, actors.

Lowell (Old French) "Like a wolf cub." Lowell Thomas,

U.S. news broadcaster and writer; Lowell Weicker, Connecticut governor. **Lovell, Lowe**

Lucas (Latin) "Bearer of light." Luciano Pavarotti, opera singer. **Luca, Lucian, Luciano, Lucias, Lucien, Lucio, Lucius, Lukas, Luke**

Ludlow (Old English) "From the prince's hill."

Luke (Greek) Biblical name meaning "one from Lucania." **Luc, Lucas, Lukas, Lukus**

Luther (Old German) "Renowned warrior of the people." Name used to honor Martin Luther, religious reformer and translator of the Bible. More recently, the name is associated with Martin Luther King, Jr. **Lothaire, Lothario, Lutero**

Lyle (Old French) "From the island." **Lyell**

Lyman (Old English) "A man from the valley." Lyman Abbott, religious leader and editor; Lyman Frank Baum, author of *The Wizard of Oz*.

Lyn (Welsh) "One who lives near the lake or waterfall." Lyn Swann, football player. **Llyn, Lynn**

Lyndon (Old English) "From the hill with the linden or lime tree." Lyndon B. Johnson, thirty-sixth U.S. president. **Linden, Lindon, Lynden**

BOYS
M

Maas (Dutch) "A twin." Short form of Thomas.

Mac (Scottish Gaelic) "The son of." **Mack**

Macadam (Scottish Gaelic) "Adam's son."

Macaulay (Scottish Gaelic) "Son of the ancestor." Macaulay Culkin, actor. **Macauley, Macawley**

Mackenzie (Irish Gaelic) "The leader or ruler's son." **McKenzie**

Mackinley (Irish Gaelic) "The learned ruler's son." **McKinley**

Maddock (Old Welsh) "One who performs acts of kindness." Ford Maddox Ford, writer. **Maddox, Madoc, Madock**

Madison (Old English) "The skillful soldier's son." James Madison, fourth U.S. president. **Maddie, Maddy, Son, Sonny**

Magnus (Latin) "Great one." **Maghnes, Magnes, Manius, Manus, Mauno**

Maitland (Old English) "Dweller in the meadow."

Major (Latin) "Greater one." **Mayer, Mayor**

Malachi (Hebrew) Biblical name meaning "the Lord's messenger." A minor prophet who foretells the coming of Christ. **Malachy**

Malak (Arabic) "An angel." **Malek, Malik**

Malcolm (Latin) "Dovelike one." (Scottish Gaelic) "One who is devoted to St. Columba." Malcolm X, civil rights leader; Malcolm Forbes, magazine publisher. **Calum, Colm, Mal**

Mallory (Old French) "Unfortunate one." (Old German) "A war counselor." **Malory**

Mandel (German) "A man." Mandy Patinkin, actor. **Mandy, Mannie, Manny**

Manfred (Old German) "A mighty peacemaker." **Fred, Freddie, Freddy, Manfredo, Manfried, Manfrid**

Manley (Old English) "Of the meadow shared among men." **Mannie, Manny**

Manning (Old English) "Son of a mighty man."

Manuel (Spanish) "One whom God is with." Form of Emmanuel. Manny Mota and Manny Sanguille, baseball players. **Mannie, Manny**

Marcel (French) Form of Marco, Mark. Marcel Duchamp, French artist; Marcello Mastroianni, Italian actor; Marcel Proust, writer. **Mairsile, Marcelle, Marcello, Marcellus, Marcelo**

Marcus (Latin) "Little, strong one." Marc Chagall and Mark Rothko, painters; Mark Harmon, actor; Marcus Garvy, racial activist; Marco Polo, world traveler; Mark Twain, writer. **Marc, Marcello, Marcelo, Marco, Mark, Markus**

Mario (Latin) "Descended from or associated with Mars, the Roman god of war." Mario Andretti, car racer; Mario Cuomo, New York State governor. **Marion, Marius**

Marley (Old English) "Of the meadow filled with water." **Marland**

Marlon (French) "Like a small falcon." Marlon Brando, actor. **Marlin, Merlin**

Marlow (Old English) "Of the lakeside hill." **Marlowe**

Marshall (Old German)"One who cares for the horses." Marshall Field, merchant and philanthropist. **Mars, Marshal**

Martin (Latin) "One who is associated with Mars, the Roman god of war." Martin Luther, religious reformer; Martin Van Buren, eighth U.S. president; Martin Luther King, Jr., civil rights leader; Martin Scorsese, movie director; Martin Sheen, actor. **Mart, Martainn, Marten, Martie, Martino, Marton, Marty, Martyn**

Marvin (Middle English) "Heroic friend." Marvin Gaye, popular singer; Marvin Hamlisch, songwriter. **Marven, Marwin**

Mason (Old French) "One who works with stone." **Maison, Mayson, Sonnie, Sonny**

Matthew (Hebrew) Biblical name meaning "a gift of God." Matthew Broderick and Matt Dillon, actors. **Maitias, Mateo, Mateus, Mathe, Mathew, Mathian, Mathias, Mathies, Mathieu, Mats, Matt, Matthiew, Mattie, Matty, Mayhew**

Maurice (Latin) "One with a dark complexion." Maurice Chevalier, actor. **Mauricio, Maurits, Morey, Moritz, Morris, Morry, Morse, Moss**

Maximilian (Latin) "The greatest, most famous one." Max Ernst, French painter. **Mac, Mack, Massimiliano, Max, Maxie, Maxim, Maximilien, Maximo, Maximus**

Maxwell (Old English) "From Mack's stream." Maxwell Perkins, book editor. **Mac, Max**

Maynard (Old German) "One who is strong and brave." **Mayne, Meinard, Menard**

Mead (Old English) "From the clearing." **Meade**

Meir (Hebrew) "One who gives light." Meyer Lansky, Mafia leader; Meyer Schapiro, art historian. **Maier, Mayer, Mayr, Meier, Meyer, Myer**

Melbourne (Old English) "From near the millstream." **Melburn, Milburn**

Melville (Old English) "A hard worker." Mel Brooks, filmmaker; Mel Gibson, actor. **Mel, Melvin, Melvyn**

Mendel (Hebrew) "Wise comforter." Menachem Begin, prime minister of Israel. **Menachem, Menahem**

Mercer (Middle English) "A merchant who sells fabrics." Merce Cunningham, dancer and choreographer. **Merce**

Merle (Old French) "Like a blackbird." Merle Haggard, country and western singer.

Merrick (Old English) "A hardworking leader." **Mayrick, Merick, Rick**

Merrill (Old French) "Famous one." **Merill, Merrel, Merrell, Merritt, Meryl**

Merton (Old English) "One who lives near a lake." **Merten, Murton**

Mervyn (Welsh) "From the hill by the sea." Name of the wizard in King Arthur's court. Merv Griffin, TV talk show host. **Merlin, Merlyn, Merv, Merwin, Murvyn, Myrvyn, Myrwin**

Michael (Hebrew) "One who is like God." Michael Jackson, singer; Mickey Rooney, Michael Douglas, and Michael J. Fox, actors; Mikhail Baryshnikov, dancer; Michelangelo Buonarroti, painter; Mickey Mantle, baseball player; Mike Nichols, movie director; Mick Jagger, rock 'n' roll star. **Micah, Michal, Michail, Michelangelo, Mick, Mickey, Mickie, Miguel, Mikael, Mike, Mikhail, Mischa, Misha, Mitch, Mitchel, Mitchell, Mychal**

Middleton (Old English) "From the farm or town in the middle of others."

Milburn (Old English) "From the stream near the mill."

Miles (Latin) "A soldier." Miles Standish, American colonist. **Mills, Milo, Myles**

Millard (Old English) "Caretaker of the mill." (Old French) "Strong, flattering one." Millard Fillmore, thirteenth U.S. president. **Miller, Milo, Milward**

Milton (Old English) "From the town with a mill." Milton Avery, painter; Milton Berle, comedian. **Milt, Miltie, Milty**

Miner (Old French) "One who works in the mines." (Latin) "A youth." **Minor**

Mitch (Middle English) Form of Michael. **Mitchel, Mitchell**

Monroe (Irish Gaelic) "From near the mouth of the red, swampy river." James Monroe, fifth U.S. president. **Monro, Monrow, Munro, Munroe**

Montague (French) "From the peaked mountain area." Became an aristocratic British name after the Norman Conquest. Monty Hall, TV game show host. **Montagu, Monte, Monty**

Montgomery (Old English) "From the landowner's estate on the hill." Montgomery Clift, actor. **Gomer, Monte, Monty**

Moore (Old French) "Darkly complected one." (Middle English) "From the moor." **Moreland, Morland**

Mordecai (Persian) Biblical name meaning "devoted to the god Marduk." **Mord, Mort, Mortie, Motke, Motl**

Morey (Welsh) form of Maurice. **Morie, Morrie, Morry**

Morgan (Old Welsh) "One who lives by the sea." **Morgen, Morgun**

Morley (Old English) "From the clearing on the moor." **Morlee, Morlie**

Morris (Old English) Form of Maurice. Morris West, Australian writer. **Moris, Morrison, Morse**

Mortimer (Old French) "From near the stagnant body of water." **Mort, Morty**

Morton (Old English) "From the town on the moor." **Mort, Morten, Morty**

Moses (Egyptian) "Child born of God." (Hebrew) "One who is saved." Biblical prophet responsible for leading the Israelites out of Egypt and for giving them the Ten Commandments. Moss Hart, playwright and director. **Moe, Moishe, Moshe, Moss**

Muhammad (Arabic) "Praised one." Muhammad was the founder of the Muslim religion. **Ahmad, Hamid, Hammad, Mahmud, Mohammad**

Muir (Scottish Gaelic) "From the moor."

Murdoch (Irish Gaelic) "Sea warrior or sailor." **Murdo, Murdock, Murdy**

Murphy (Irish Gaelic) "A man of the sea." **Murph, Murphie**

Murray (Scottish Gaelic) "One who is seaworthy." **Moray, Murrey, Murry**

Myron (Greek) "From a sweet-smelling oil (myrrh)." It is associated with the gift of myrrh given to the baby Jesus by one of the three wise men. **My, Ron, Ronnie, Ronny**

BOYS
N

Nahum (Hebrew) Biblical name meaning "one who comforts or consoles." Prophet who foretells the fall of Nineveh." **Nahman, Naum**

Nando (Italian) "Bold adventurer." Form of Ferdinand. **Nandel, Nandru**

Naphtali (Hebrew) Biblical name meaning "one worth wrestling for." Name of one of the sons of Jacob and Rebecca.

Napier (Old English) "One who makes napery or linens."

Napoleon (Greek) "Like a lion from the woods." (Italian) "One from Naples." Napoleon Bonaparte, French emperor. **Leon, Napoleone**

Nager (Hebrew) "A carpenter." **Neiger, Nuger**

Narcissus (Greek) "Full of self-love." In classical mythology, Narcissus is a beautiful boy who falls in love with his own reflection in a pond. Unable to pull himself away, he eventually turns into a flower (the narcissus). **Narcis, Narcisco, Narcisse**

Nathan (Hebrew) Biblical name meaning "a gift." Nat King Cole, singer. **Nat, Nate**

Nathaniel (Hebrew) Biblical name meaning "a gift given of God." Nathaniel Hawthorne, author of *The Scarlett Letter*. Nathaniel West, writer. **Nat, Nataniel, Nate, Nathanael, Nathanial**

Neal (Irish Gaelic) "A winner, champion." O'Neill is an Irish clan name. Neil Armstrong, astronaut; Neil Diamond, singer; Neil Simon, playwright; Neil Young and Nils Loffgren, musicians. **Neale, Neall, Neel, Neil, Neill, Neils, Nels, Nial, Niels, Nil, Niles, Nils**

Ned (English) "Guardian of one's wealth." Short form of Edward.

Nehemiah (Hebrew) Biblical name meaning "one whom God comforts." **Hemiah, Nehem**

■ NICKNAMES ■

Elizabeth or Betsy? What's in a Nickname?

Americans love nicknames. They give them to their husbands, wives, sons, daughters, friends, and enemies. A nickname can be endearing or sarcastic; shorter than a given name or longer. It can describe a physical aspect, such as Red for someone with red hair, or an intangible characteristic such as Magic for a professional basketball player known for his finesse (Earvin Johnson).

No matter how hard you try to avoid having your darling Elizabeth called Beth or Betty or Betsy or Lizzie, chances are she will be called by at least one of these nicknames. So if you don't like the nicknames for a name you're considering, keep searching.

Here are some nicknames and the famous people who have lived with them:

Babe	George Herman Ruth, baseball player
Bojangles	Bill Robinson, tap dancer and actor
Buggsy	Benjamin Segal, mobster
Chevy	Cornelius Crane Chase, comedian
Ike	Dwight David Eisenhower, thirty-fourth U.S. president
Jake	Jack Kramer, tennis player
Jimbo	Jimmy Connors, tennis player
The Juice	O. J. Simpson, football player
Lady Bird	Mrs. Lyndon Baines Johnson, First Lady
Pearl	Janis Joplin, pop singer
Punch	Arthur Ochs Sulzberger, owner of *The New York Times*
Ringo	Richard Starkey, drummer for the Beatles
Rocky	Nelson A. Rockefeller, governor of New York and forty-first U.S. vice president
Scoop	Henry Jackson, U.S. senator from Washington State
Sissy	Mary Elizabeth Spacek, actress
Slim	Lady Nancy Keith, socialite
Sting	Gordon Summer, rock singer
Swifty	Irving Paul Lazar, Hollywood agent
Telly	Aristotle Savalas, actor

Tip	Thomas P. O'Neill, Jr., Speaker of the U.S. House of Representatives
Yogi	Lawrence Peter Berra, baseball player
Zsa Zsa	Sari Gabor, actress

Nelson (Scandinavian) "Son of the champion." Nelson Doubleday, co-owner of the New York Mets; Nelson Eddy, singer and actor; Nelson Rockefeller governor of New York and forty-first U.S. vice president. **Nealson, Nels, Nils, Nilson**

Nemo (Greek) "Of the glade."

Nero (Latin) "One who is stern or strict." **Neron, Nerone**

Nester (Greek) "Wise traveler." **Nestor, Nestore**

Neville (Old French) "From the new village." Neville Chamberlain, British prime minister. **Nevil, Nevile**

Nevin (Irish Gaelic) "Worshiper of the holy." (Old English) "A nephew." **Nevan, Nevins, Niven**

Newell (Old English) "From the new hall or manor house." **Newall**

Newman (Old English) "A newcomer."

Newton (Old English) "From the new town."

Nicholas (Greek) "Of the victorious people." St. Nicholas is the patron saint of children and also known as Santa Claus. Nicholas Cage and Nick Nolte, actors. **Claus, Cole, Colin, Klaus, Kolya, Niccolo, Nichol, Nick, Nickie, Nickolaus, Nicky, Nicol, Nicolas, Nicolo, Niki, Nikki, Niklaus, Nikolai, Nikolos, Nikos, Nikta, Niles, Nils**

Nicodemus (Greek) "Conqueror of the people." **Nicodeme, Nicodemo, Nicomedo**

Nicolson (Greek) "Son of Nicholas." **Nicholson, Nikolson**

Nigel (Latin) "Black or dark-haired one." (Irish Gaelic) "A champion." **Nye, Nygel**

Nixon (Old English) "Son of Nicholas." **Nickson, Nicson**

Noah (Hebrew) Biblical name meaning "to rest and take comfort in." Noah built the ark and gathered aboard two of each living creature. Noah Webster, author of *American Dictionary of the English Language.* **Noach, Noak, Noé**

Noam (Hebrew) "Joyful, delightful one." Noam Chomsky, linguist.

Noble (Latin) "Of noble birth." **Nobel, Nobie, Noby**

Noel, Noël (Latin) "One born on Christmas." Noël Coward, English actor. **Nowell**

Nolan (Irish Gaelic) "Nobleman." Nolan Ryan, baseball player. **Noland, Nolen**

Norbert (Old Norse) "Brilliant hero."

Norman (Old English) "One from the North." Norman Mailer, writer; Norman Rockwell, illustrator; H. Norman Schwarzkopf, American general. **Norm, Normand, Normie, Normy**

Norris (French) Form of Norman. Norris McWhirter, editor of *The Guinness Book of World Records*. **Noris, Norrie, Norry**

Northrop (Old English) "From the northernmost farm." **North, Northrup**

Norton (Old English) "From the northern town."

Norville (Old English) "From the northern village." **Norval, Norvel**

Norwood (Old English) "From the north woods." **Norvin, Norward**

Nowles (Middle English) "From the grass-covered slope in the woods." **Knolls, Knowles**

Nuri (Hebrew) "My fire." **Nur, Nuria, Nuriel**

Nye (Middle English) "From the island."

Boys
O

Oakes (Old English) "From the area surrounded by oak trees." **Oak, Oaks**

Obadiah (Hebrew) Biblical name meaning "the Lord's servant." **Obadias, Obie, Oby, Ovadia**

Octavius (Latin) "The eighth." Often used for the eighth child born. **Octave, Octavian, Octavus, Tavey, Tavie**

Odell (Middle English) "From the wooded hill." (Scandinavian) "One who is small but wealthy." **Dell, Ode, Odey, Odie**

Oen (Welsh) "Lamblike."

Ogden (Old English) "From the valley of oak trees." Ogden Nash, writer. **Ogdan, Ogdon**

Ogilvie (Old English) "From the high plain." **Ogilvey, Ogilvy**

Olaf (Scandinavian) "Descended from an ancestor." In Norway, the name of five kings. **Ola, Olav, Ole, Olen, Oli, Olin, Oluf, Olov, Olovi**

Oleg (Russian) "Holy one." Oleg Cassini, fashion designer.

Oliver (Latin) "From the olive tree," probably referring to the olive tree as a symbol of peace. Oliver Cromwell, English general and statesman; Oliver Wendell Holmes, justice of the U.S. Supreme Court. **Noll, Olivero, Olivier, Oliviero, Ollie, Olly, Olvan**

Omar (Hebrew) Biblical name meaning "eloquent one." (Arabic) "One who follows the Prophet." Omar Sharif, actor. **Omer**

Omri (Hebrew) Biblical name of a king of Israel meaning "from a sheaf of wheat." **Omer**

Oren (Hebrew) "From the pine trees." (Irish Gaelic) "Pale or fair in complexion." **Oran, Orin, Orren, Orrin**

Orestes (Greek) "Man of the mountains." In Greek mythology, Orestes was the son of Agamemnon. **Oreste**

Orion (Greek) "Son of the one with light or fire." In Greek mythology, Orion was the hunter who was slain by Artemis and turned into a big constellation in the sky.

Orlando (Italian) "One who is famous throughout the land." Form of Roland. Name of a book by Virginia Woolf; Orlando Cepeda, baseball player. **Lannie, Lanny, Orlan, Orland**

Orpheus (Greek) "Charming one." In classical Greek mythology, Orpheus, a beautiful musician, descends to the underworld in search of his dead wife. He charms Hades, king of the underworld, with his music and thus is given his wife back. **Orfeo**

Orrick (Old English) "From near the old oak tree." Oral Roberts, evangelist. **Oral, Orrie, Orry, Rick**

Orson (Latin) "Like a bear cub." Orson Welles, actor. **Ors, Sonny, Urson**

Orville (French) "From the estate or village of gold." Orville Wright, aviation pioneer. **Orv, Orval, Orvil**

Osborn (Scandinavian) "Divine, bearlike one." (Old English) "A divine warrior." **Osborne, Osbourn, Osbourne, Ozzie, Ozzy**

Oscar (Irish Gaelic) "Fast and quiet like a deer." (Scandinavian) "Godlike spearman." Oscar Wilde, writer and wit; Oscar Hammerstein, lyric writer. **Osgar, Oskar, Oskari, Ossie, Ozzy**

Osgood (Old English) "One with divine goodness." **Ozzi, Ozzy**

Osmond (Old English) "Godlike protector." **Esme, Osman, Osmund, Ozzy**

Ossian (Irish Gaelic) "Fawnlike." **Oisein, Osheen**

Oswald (Old English) "One who is all-powerful." **Ossie, Oswalt, Oswell, Ozzie, Waldo**

Oswin (Old English) "Friend of God." **Oswyn**

Otis (Greek) "One possessed with unusual powers of healing." (Old English) "Son of Otto." Otis Redding, soul singer. **Oates, Otes, Otilio**

Otmar (Old German) "Wealthy, illustrious one."

Otto (Old German) "Wealthy one." A modern form of Odo. Otto the Great; Otto Rank, Austrian psychologist. **Odon, Odt, Otello, Othello, Oto, Otte, Tilo**

Owen (Latin) "Nobly born one." (Welsh) Form of Evan meaning "lamblike or young warrior." **Ewen, Owain**

Oxford (Old English) "From the place near the river where oxen cross." **Ford**

Boys
P

Pablo (Spanish) Form of Paul. Pablo Picasso, painter.

Paco (Spanish) Form of Francisco.

Paddy (Irish) Form of Patrick. Paddy has come to be a generic nickname for an Irishman.

Page (French) "A nobleman's servant." **Padget, Padgett, Paget, Paige**

Paine (Latin) "From the countryside." **Payne**

Palmer (Old English) "One who carries a palm." Often used for boys who are born on Palm Sunday. **Palme**

Pancho (Spanish) Form of Francisco. Pancho Gonzales, tennis player; Pancho Villa, Mexican revolutionary leader. **Paco, Paquito**

Paris (Greek) "A journeyman." In classical Greek mythology it is Paris who carries off Helene from Sparta, causing the Trojan War. **Parris**

Parker (Middle English) "A keeper of the park." **Park, Parke, Parks**

Parnell (Old French) "A small Peter." **Parrnell, Pernell, Perrin.**

Parrish (Middle English) "From the church or parish yard." **Parrie, Parry**

Pascal (French) "One born on Easter or Passover." **Pace, Pascale, Pascual, Pasquale**

Pastor (Latin) "A shepherd."

Patrick (Latin) "A nobleman or patrician." St. Patrick is the patron saint of Ireland. Pat Boone, singer; Patrick Swayze, actor. **Paddie, Paddy, Padraic, Padraig, Padriac, Pat, Paton, Patric, Patrice, Patricio, Patten, Patton**

Paul (Latin) Biblical name meaning "small one." Name of the saint who is said to have cofounded the Christian Church with St. Peter. Paul Revere, American patriot; Paul Cézanne, French painter; Paul McCartney and Paul Simon, singers and songwriters; Paul Newman, actor. **Pablo, Pall, Paolo, Pasha, Paulie, Paulin, Pauls, Pauly, Pavel, Pavlik, Poul**

Paxton (Old English) "From the town where peace reigns." **Packston, Pax, Paxon**

Pedro (Spanish) Form of Peter.

Pelham (Old English) "From the homestead of the Peolas," referring to a distinguished English family's home. Pelham Grenville (P. G.) Wodehouse, English novelist.

Pembroke (Welsh) "From the promontory." **Brook, Pembrook**

Penrod (Old German) "Famous leader." **Pen, Penn, Rod, Roddie, Roddy**

Pepito (Spanish) "God shall add." Form of Joseph. **José, Pepe**

Percival (Old French) "One who pierces or breaks through the valley." Sir Percival, a knight of King Arthur's Round Table. **Parsefal, Parsifal, Pearcy, Perce, Perceval, Perci, Percy, Purcell**

Perry (Middle English) "From near the pear trees." (Old French) Form of Peter. **Parry, Pere**

Peter (Greek) "Stone or rocklike." St. Peter is one of Christ's twelve Apostles and considered to be a cofounder of the Christian Church. Peter Pan, the main character of James Barrie's captivating tale. Piet Mondrian, Dutch painter; Peter Max, pop artist; Pete Rose, baseball player; Pete Seeger, folk singer; Peter Sellers, actor. **Farris, Ferris, Panos, Parry, Peadar, Pearce, Peder, Pedr, Pedro, Peirce, Per, Pere, Perkin, Perren, Perrin, Petar, Pete, Petey, Petie, Petre, Petro, Pierce, Pierre, Pierrot, Piers, Piet, Pieter, Pietro, Pyotr**

Peyton (Old English) "From the estate of the warrior." Peyton Randolph, president of the first American Congress. **Pate, Payton**

Philip (Greek) Biblical name meaning "one who loves horses." St. Philip, one of Christ's twelve Apostles. Phil Collins, popular singer and songwriter; Phil Donahue, TV personality; Phillip Johnson, architect; Philip Roth, American novelist. **Felipe, Filip, Filppo, Flip, Phelps, Phil, Philipp, Philippos, Phillip, Phillips, Phipp, Pip**

Phineas (Hebrew) Biblical name meaning "from the oracle." Phineas Taylor (P. T.) Barnum, cofounder of Barnum & Bailey Circus. **Phinneas, Pinchas, Pincus, Pinhaus**

Pierce (English) Form of Peter. **Pearce**

Pierre (French) Form of Peter. Pierre Franey, chef and cookbook writer; Pierre Salinger, journalist.

Piran (Welsh) "Black one." The name of a Cornish saint who is the patron saint of miners. **Peran, Pieran**

Placido (Latin) "Untroubled one." Placido Domingo, opera singer. **Placide**

Plato (Greek) "Strong, broad-shouldered one." The name of a famous ancient greek philosopher. **Platon**

Pomeroy (Old French) "From near the apple orchard." **Pomer, Pommie, Pommy, Roy**

Porter (Latin) "A doorman or gatekeeper." **Port**

Powell (Welsh) "One who is alert." **Howell, Powel**

Prentice (Latin) "An apprentice." **Prent, Prentis**

Prescott (Old English) "Of the priest's cottage." **Prest, Scott, Scottie, Scotty**

Presley (Old English) "From the priest's meadow." **Pressley, Priestley, Priestly**

Preston (Old English) "From the town with a priest."

Price (Welsh) "Son of the passionate, ardent one." **Brice, Bryce, Pryce**

Primo (Latin) "Firstborn." **Prym**

Prince (Latin) "Princelike." Prince, rock musician. **Prinz**

Proctor (Latin) "One who administers." **Procter, Prockter**

Prosper (Latin) "Fortunate or prosperous." **Prospero**

Pryor (Latin) "Superior one" or "head of a priory." **Prior, Pry, Prye**

Putnam (Old English) "From near the pond." **Putnem**

BOYS
Q

Quartus (Latin) "The fourth one."

Quentin (Latin) "The fifth one." Quentin Bell, nephew and biographer of Virginia Woolf. **Quent, Quinn, Quint, Quintin, Quintus, Quito**

Quillan (Irish Gaelic) "Cublike."

Quimby (Scandinavian) "From the estate of a woman." **Quim, Quin, Quinby**

Quincy (Old French) "From the estate of the fifth son." John Quincy Adams, sixth U.S. president; Quincy Jones, musician. **Quinn, Quinzee, Quinzey**

Quinlan (Irish Gaelic) "One with great physical strength." **Quinley, Quinlin, Quinlyn**

Quinn (Irish Gaelic) "Keen or wise one."

Quinton (Old English) "From the estate of the queen."

■ PLAY BALL! ■

Okay, let's say that your baby has been born and you are resting comfortably, except for your growing desperation to find a name for the baby. Your husband has left the hospital to walk around the block, and you are supposed to be asleep. But you can't sleep, because you need an idea—your family names are out, his family names are out, and you just can't take one more argument about this name business.

One strategy might be to go with sports, especially

if you are married to a fan. And if the suggestion comes from you, your partner will be pleasantly surprised.

So, arranged by sport, here is a list of some all-time greats. Lets hope you like their names:

Baseball

Ty Cobb. The greatest hitter in the history of the game. But who ever thought of calling a baby "Ty"?

Babe Ruth. The greatest of all time. Luckily, you have a choice here between Babe or George Herman, the Sultan of Swat's real given names.

Mickey Mantle. The most beloved hitter when most baby boomers were kids. So you want to call your son "Mickey"? Fine.

Football

Vince Lombardi Pro football's greatest coach ever. Definitely a name that bucks a trend these days.

O. J. Simpson. One of the game's greatest running backs. But his real first name is Orenthal. Good luck.

Joe Namath. The New York Jets' great quarterback, and a very attractive guy. Actually, there are lots of other great Joes in sports; take your pick: DiMaggio, Louis, Montana, etc. Just tell your husband you want to name junior after the greatest athlete who ever lived. Joe.

Hockey

Wayne Gretzky. The greatest hockey player of all time. He was a franchise player for the Edmonton Oilers but recently defected to the Los Angeles Kings.

Phil Esposito. A great scorer on the Boston Bruins and later the New York Rangers; now a hockey executive. Esposito won the Ross Trophy (for scoring) in 1969 and 1971–74 and the Hart Memorial Trophy (for most valuable player) in 1969 and 1974.

Bobby Orr. Part of a potent scoring combo with Esposito on the Bruins. Orr won the Ross Trophy in 1970 and 1975 and the Hart Memorial Trophy in 1970–72.

Basketball

Wilt Chamberlain Greatest player of his era and the first truly great tall center.

Kareem Abdul-Jabbar (but he started out as Lew Alcindor). Wilt's natural successor, recently retired after one of the longest and most distinguished careers in the game.

Larry Bird. The greatest white player of his era, perhaps of any era.

Golf

Jack Nicklaus. "The Golden Bear." Some say the greatest golfer in history.

Ben Hogan. The greatest American golfer of his era. Winner of four U.S. Opens, two Masters, one British Open.

Arnold Palmer. The first player to show that professional golf could be a big-money game.

Tennis

Arthur Ashe. One of America's tennis greats, certainly the greatest black player in the history of the game. Won the U.S. Open in 1968, Wimbledon in 1975. After retirement, one of the great coaches in the game.

Jimmy Connors. Played in the semifinals of the U.S. Open on his fortieth birthday, a nearly superhuman feat. Unfortunately, he lost.

John McEnroe. The *enfant terrible* of tennis in the 1980s and still one of the game's most colorful players. The other tennis McEnroe is John's younger brother Patrick.

Boxing

Muhammad Ali (Cassius Clay). The most controversial boxer of his era.

Sugar Ray Robinson. A great welterweight and middleweight from the 1940s and 1950s.

Joe Louis. The greatest American boxer of the pre-World War II era.

BOYS
R

Radburn (Old English) "One who lives near the red stream." **Burney, Burnie, Rad, Radborn, Radbourne**

Radcliffe (Old English) "From the settlement near a red cliff." **Cliff, Rad, Radcliff, Raddie, Raddy**

Radley (Old English) "From the red meadow."

Radnor (Old English) "From the red shore."

Rafferty (Irish Gaelic) "Prosperous and wealthy." **Rafe, Raff, Raffarty**

Rafi (Arabic) "Exalted one." Raffi, children's singer. **Raffi, Raffin**

Rainer (Old German) "Decisive warrior." **Raine, Rainerio, Rainier, Ranier, Raynor, Regnier**

Raleigh (Old English) "From the valley full of deer." **Lee, Leigh, Rawl, Rawley**

Ralph (Old English) "A fierce warrior or counselor." Ralph Waldo Emerson, philosopher and poet. **Rafe, Raff, Ralf, Raoul, Raul, Rolf, Rolfe, Rolph**

Ralston (Old English) "From the estate of Ralph." **Ralfston**

Ramsay (Old English) "From the island populated with rams." J. Ramsay MacDonald, British prime minister. **Ram, Ramsden, Ramsey**

Randall (Middle English) Form of Randolph. **Rand, Randal, Randel, Randell, Randi, Randie, Randle, Randol, Randy**

Randolph (Old English) "Protected by wolves." William Randolph Hearst, publisher. **Rand, Randall, Randolf, Randy**

Ransom (Old English) "Son of the shield."

Raoul (French) Form of Ralph and Randolph. Raoul Dufy, French painter; Raul Julia, actor. **Raul**

Raphael (Hebrew) Biblical name meaning "one who heals with the guidance of God." Raffaello Santi, famous Italian painter. **Rafael, Rafaelle, Rafe, Rafer, Raffaele, Raffaello, Ray**

Rashid (Swahili) "Wise advisor." **Rasheed**

Rastus (Latin) "One who loves." Form of Erastus.

Ravi (Hindu) "Sun." **Ravid, Raviv**

Rawlins (Old English-French) "Son of the wise, wolflike one." **Rawson**

Ray (Old French) "Decisionmaker or king." Also a short form of Raymond. Ray Bolger, actor; Ray Bradbury, science-fiction writer; Ray Charles, singer; Ray Kroc, founder of McDonald's restaurants.

Rayburn (Old English) "From the deer stream." **Rayfield, Rayford**

Raymond (Old German) "A wise and mighty protector." Raymond Burr, actor; Raymond Chandler, novelist. **Raimondo, Raimund, Raimundo, Ramon, Ramond, Ray, Raymund, Reamonn**

Raynor (Old Norse) "Mighty army." **Ragnar, Rainer, Ray, Rayner**

Read (Old English) "Red-haired or red-complected one." Originated as a nickname much like we use "Red." **Reade, Reed, Reid**

Redding (Old English) "Son of the red-haired one." **Reading**

Redford (Old English) "From the crossing in the red river." **Ford, Radford, Red, Redd**

Rees (Welsh) "Ardent, passionate one." Traditional Welsh name. Rhett Butler, dashing character in *Gone With the Wind*. **Reece, Reese, Rhett, Rhys, Rice**

Reeve (Middle English) "Manager of an estate or farm." **Reave, Reeves**

Regan (Irish Gaelic) "Descended from the little king." From the Irish last name O'Riagain. **Reagan, Reagen, Regen**

Reginald (Old English) "A powerful ruler." Reggie Jackson, baseball player; Regis Philbin, TV talk show cohost. **Reggie, Reggy, Reginauld, Regis, Reinald, Reinhold, Renault, Rene, Reynold, Reynolds, Rinaldo**

Remington (Old English) "From the raven's town or estate." **Remy, Tony**

Remus (Latin) "Quick-moving one." The legendary brothers Remus and Romulus founded the city of Rome. Uncle Remus is the narrator of the *Uncle Remus Stories* by Joel Chandler. **Remigio, Remo, Remy**

Renault (French) Form of Reginald. **Renaud, René**

René (French) "One who is born again." **Renat, Renate, Renato, Renny**

Reuben (Hebrew) Biblical name meaning "behold, a son is born." Reuben is the oldest son of Jacob. **Reuban, Reubin, Rube, Ruben, Rubin, Ruby, Rueben**

Reuel (Hebrew) Biblical name meaning "a friend to God."

Rex (Latin) "The all-powerful king." Rex Harrison, actor. **Rey, Roi**

Reynard (Old German) "Powerful warrior." **Ranard, Raynard, Reinhard, Reinhardt, Renard, Renaud, Renard**

Rhodes (Old English) "From Rhodes." (Greek) "From the place of roses." **Rodes**

Richard (Old German) "The all-powerful ruler." The name of three kings of England, starting with Richard the Lion-Hearted (1157–99); Richard Burton, Richard Chamberlain, Richard Dreyfuss, and Richard Harris, actors; Richard Avedon, photographer; Dick Cavett, TV personality; Richard Pryor, comedian. **Dick, Dickie, Dicky, Ricard, Ricardo, Riccardo, Rich, Richardo, Richart, Richie, Richy, Rick, Ricki, Rickie, Rico, Riki, Ritchie**

■ PERSONAL HERITAGE ■

Names are meant to identify who we are and where we came from. So what could be more appropriate in a name search than going back to our roots? Of course, in America there are many strange ethnic name combinations. Where else would you find a Latoya Valencia or a Yi Chang Edelstein?

Perhaps your family would be pleased if you named a son after your recently deceased grandpa, Moses. But keep in mind that it might sound funny with your husband's Celtic last name. Moses Pembroke doesn't have the same ring as, say, Morey (a form of Seymour) Pembroke. You'll have to decide how much of your child's name you want to reflect your and your husband's roots. Remember, whatever name you choose will affect your child's self-image, so make sure you're proud of it before passing it along.

Richmond (Old German) "All-powerful guardian." **Richman, Richmound**

Ridgley (Old English) "From the valley ridge." **Ridge, Ridley**

Rigby (Old English) "From the valley of the all-powerful."

Riley (Irish Gaelic) "Brave, valiant one." **Reilly**

Ring (Old English) "Ring." **Ringo**

Riordan (Irish Gaelic) "A royal poet or bard." **Dan, Dannie, Danny, Reardan, Rearden**

Rip (Dutch) "Full-grown or ripe." Rip Van Winkle, character created by Washington Irving.

Ripley (Old English) "From the shouter's clearing." **Lee, Leigh, Rip**

Rivers (Latin) "Stream of water." River Phoenix, actor. **River**

Roald (Scandinavian) "Famous ruler." Roald Amundsen, polar explorer who discovered the South Pole.

Roarke (Irish Gaelic) "Illustrious ruler." **Rorke, Rourke**

Robert (Old German) "Brilliant, famous one." Robert E. Lee, Confederate general; Robert Frost, American poet; Robert DeNiro, Rob Lowe, Robert Redford, and Robert Wagner, actors. **Bob, Bobbie, Bobby, Rip, Rob, Robart, Robard, Robb, Robbie, Robby, Roberto, Robin, Rupert, Ruperto**

Robinson (Old English) "Son of Robert or Robin." Robin Hood, legendary hero; Robinson Crusoe, main character in the novel of the same name by Daniel Defoe; Robin Williams, actor and comedian. **Robbin, Robers, Robin, Robinet**

Rocco (Old German) "One who rests." **Roch, Rock, Rocky, Rogue, Rook**

Rochester (Old English) "From the fortress built of rocks." Rock Hudson, actor. **Chester, Chet, Roch, Rock, Rocky**

Rockwell (Old English) "From the rocky stream."

Roderick (Old German) "Famous ruler." Roddy McDowell, actor; Rod Stewart, rock singer. **Rod, Rodd, Roddie, Roddy, Roderic, Roderich, Roderigo, Rodrick, Rodrigo, Rodrique, Rorey, Rory, Rurik, Ruy**

Rodney (Old English) "A new and illustrious power." Rodney Dangerfield, comedian; Rod Laver, tennis player. **Rod, Rodd, Roddie, Roddy, Rodie**

Rogan (Irish Gaelic) "Red-haired one."

Roger (Old German) "Famous, brilliant with a spear." Roger Daltry, rock musician. **Roar, Rodge, Rodger, Rog, Rogerio, Rogers, Rutger**

Roland (Old German) "Famous across the land." Roland Barthes, literary critic. **Orland, Orlando, Rolando, Rolant, Roldan, Rollin, Rollins, Rollo, Rowe, Rowland**

Romeo (Italian) "One who visits Rome." Romeo is the hero of Shakespeare's romantic tragedy *Romeo and Juliet.* As a result of the play's popularity, Romeo had come to mean "a young lover." Roman Polanski, Polish movie director. **Roman, Rome**

Romney (Welsh) "From near the winding river."

Ronald (Scottish) Form of Reginald. Ron Howard and Ron Silver, actors. **Ron, Ronnie, Ronny**

Ronan (Irish Gaelic) "Like a young seal." **Rowan, Rowen**

Roosevelt (Dutch) "From the field of rose bushes." The name is given in honor of Theodore Roosevelt and Franklin Delano Roosevelt, twenty-sixth and thirty-second U.S. presidents, respectively.

Roper (Old English) "One who makes ropes."

Rory (Irish Gaelic) "Red King."

Roscoe (Scandinavian) "Swift as the forest deer." **Rosco, Ross**

Ross (Scottish Gaelic) "From the headland or peninsula." Ross McWhirter, coeditor of *The Guinness Book of World Records.* Scottish clan name. **Rosse, Rossie, Rossy**

Roth (Old German) "Red-haired one."

Rowan (Irish Gaelic) "Little red-haired one." **Rooney, Rowe, Rowen, Rowney**

Roy (Old French) "The king." Roy Lichtenstein, U.S. painter; Roy Orbison, singer; Roy Rodgers, entertainer; Roy Scheider, actor. **Roi**

Royal (Old French) "Royal." **Royall**

Royce (Old English) "The king's son." **Roy**

Rudolph (Old German) "Like the famed wolf." The name usually refers to someone who accomplishes a daring feat. Rudolf Nureyev, ballet dancer; Rudolph Valentino, actor; Rudy Vallee, comedian and singer. **Raoul, Rodolph, Rodolphe, Rolf, Rolfe, Rolph, Rudolf, Rudi, Rudy**

Rudyard (Old English) "From the cleared field containing red earth." Rudyard Kipling, English author. **Rudy**

Rufus (Latin) "Red-haired."

Rupert (German) (Italian) (Spanish) Form of Robert. Rupert Murdock, newspaper publisher.

Russell (Old French) "Red-haired one." Russell Baker, journalist; Russell Wright, industrial designer, Rusty Staub, baseball player. **Russ, Rusty**

Rutherford (Old English) "From the cattle ford." Rutherford
B. Hayes, nineteenth U.S. President. **Ford**

Rutledge (Old English) "From the red pool." **Rutter**

Ryan (Irish Gaelic) "Small king." Ryan O'Neal, actor. **Rian,
Ryon, Ryun**

Ryder (Old English) "A horseman." **Rider**

BOYS
S

Sabin (Latin) "Of the Sabine people."

Sacha (Russian) "Helper of men." Form of Alexander. **Sacsha, Sasha**

Sadler (Old English) "One who makes saddles."

Salim (Arabic) "Safe, unharmed one." **Salem, Saleem, Selim**

Salvador (Latin) "Savior," referring to Christ. Salvador Dali, surrealist painter. **Sal, Salvador, Salvatore, Salvidor, Sauveur, Xavier**

Samir (Arabic) "He who keeps one company at night with lively conversation." **Sami**

Samson (Hebrew) Biblical name meaning "one the sun shines on." In the Bible, Samson was an Israelite judge known for his prodigious strength. **Sampson, Sansom, Shem**

Samuel (Hebrew) Biblical name meaning "one whom God hears," probably referring to hearing a mother's prayer for a son. Samuel Adams, American patriot; Sammy Davis, Jr., entertainer; Samuel Goldwyn, film producer; Samuel Newhouse, publisher; Sam Shepard, actor, director, and playwright. **Sam, Sammie, Sammy, Samuele, Shem, Shemie**

Sanborn (Old English) "From the settlement by the sandy brook." **Sandy, Santon**

Sancho (Spanish) "Holy one." Sancho Panza, character in Cervantes' novel *Don Quixote*. **Sauncho**

Sanders (Middle English) "Helper of mankind." Form of Alexander. **Sander, Sanderson, Sandi, Sandor, Sandy, Saunders, Saunderson**

Sanford (Old English) "From the sandy crossing in the river." Sandy Koufax, baseball player. **Ford, Sandford, Sandi, Sandy**

Santiago (Spanish) "One who is protected by St. James,"

who is one of the twelve Apostles of Christ and the patron saint of Spain. **Diego, Iago**

Santos (Spanish) "Saintlike." A name often given to a boy born on All Saints' Day. **Santo**

Sargent (Old French) "An officer." Sargent Shriver, politician; Sergio Valenti, fashion designer. **Sarge, Serge, Sergeant, Sergent, Sergio**

Saul (Hebrew) Biblical name meaning "prayed for." The biblical Saul was the first king of Israel. Saul Bellow, writer; Saul Steinberg, painter and cartoonist. **Sol, Sollie, Solly, Zol**

Saville (French) "From the estate of willow trees."

Sawyer (Middle English) "One who saws wood." **Sawyere, Soyer**

Saxon (Old German) "One with a small sword." This was the term used by the Roman conquerors for the Germans, who used extremely small swords in battle. **Sack, Saxe**

Sayer (Welsh) "A carpenter." **Saer, Sayre, Sayres**

Schuyler (Dutch) "One who is shielded." Schuyler Colfax, seventeenth U.S. vice president. **Schuler, Sky, Skylar, Skyler**

Scott (Old English) "Someone from Scotland." F. Scott Fitzgerald, writer; Scott Joplin, "ragtime" musician. **Scotti, Scottie, Scotty**

Scully (Irish Gaelic) "The town announcer or crier."

Seabert (Old English) "From the bright sea" or "a brilliant sailor." **Sebert**

Seamus (Irish Gaelic) "A supplanter." Form of James. **Seamas, Seumas, Seumus, Shamus**

Sean (Irish Gaelic) Form of John. Sean Connery and Sean Penn, actors. **Shaughn, Shaun, Shawn**

Seaton (Old English) "From the seaside town." **Seeton, Seton**

Sebastian (Latin) "Well-respected one." Sebastian Cabot, actor; Sebastian is the name of the crab in Walt Disney's movie *The Little Mermaid*. **Bastian, Bastien, Seb, Sebastiano, Sebastien**

Sedgwick (Old English) "From the victorious battlefield." **Sedgewick, Sedgley**

Seger (Old English) "A sea warrior." **Seager, Segar**

Selig (Old German) "Happy, fortunate one." **Zelig**

Selwyn (Old English) "A friend of the manor." **Selewyn, Selwin**

Septimus (Latin) "The seventh son."

Seth (Hebrew) Biblical name meaning "given or appointed one." Seth was given to Adam and Eve by God after the murder of Abel.

Seward (Old English) "One who is victorious at sea." Seward Johnson, founder of Johnson & Johnson. **Sewell, Siward**

Seymour (Old French) "A follower of St. Maur" or "one from the town of St. Maur." **Morey, Morie Morrie, Morry, Si**

Shalom (Hebrew) "Peace be with you." **Sholom, Solomon**

Shane (Irish) "God's gracious gift." **Shain, Shaine, Shayn**

Shannon (Irish Gaelic) "Small, wise one." **Shanahan, Shannan, Shanon,**

Shaw (Old English) "From the shaded grove."

Sheehan (Irish Gaelic) "Small, wise one." **Shanahan, Shannan, Shanon**

Sheffield (Old English) "From the crooked field." **Field, Sheff**

Sheldon (Old English) "From the town on the valley ledge." **Shelby, Shelley, Shelly, Shelton**

Shem (Hebrew) Biblical name meaning "renowned." The name of Noah's oldest son.

Shepley (Old English) "From the meadow full of sheep." **Shep, Shepard, Shepherd, Sheply, Shepp, Shipley**

Sherbourne (Old English) "From near the clear brook." **Sherborn, Sherburn**

Sheridan (Irish Gaelic) "Savage or wild one." **Dan, Share, Shay**

Sherlock (Old English) "Fair-haired one." Sherlock Holmes, famous detective in Sir Arthur Conan Doyle's stories. **Lock, Locke, Sherlocke, Sherr, Shurlocke**

Sherman (Old English) "A sheep shearer." Sherman McCoy, main character in *Bonfire of the Vanities* by Tom Wolfe. **Sherm**

Sherwin (Middle English) "One who runs swiftly." (Old English) "Superb friend." **Sherwyn, Sherwynd, Win, Winnie, Wyn**

Sherwood (Old English) "From the illustrious forest." Sherwood Anderson, writer. **Sherr, Sherwin, Shurwood, Wood, Woody**

Sidney (Old English) "From the meadow by the river." (Old French) "From the town of St. Denis." Sid Caesar, comedian; Sidney Sheldon, popular novelist; Sidney Poitier, actor. **Sid, Syd, Sydney**

Siegfried (Old German) "Peace reigns victorious." An important hero of old German legend. Siegfried and Roy, Las Vegas entertainment team. **Siffre, Sig, Sigfrid, Sigfried, Siggie, Siggy**

Sigmund (Old German) "Victorious protector." Sigmund Freud, psychologist. **Sig, Siggy, Sigimundo, Sigismund, Sigmond, Zig, Ziggy**

Silas (Latin) Biblical name meaning "of the forest." Silas Marner, main character of George Eliot's novel of the same name. **Si, Silvano**

Silvester (Latin) "From the woods." Sylvester Stallone, actor. **Silvestre, Sly, Slyvain, Sylvester**

Simon (Hebrew) Biblical name meaning "one who listens respectfully." **Si, Sim, Simeon, Simms, Simone, Simpson, Simson, Sy, Sym, Syman, Symon**

Sinclair (Old French) "From St. Clair." (Latin) "Illustrious one." Sinclair Lewis, novelist. **Clair, Clare, Sinclare**

Skipper (Middle Dutch) "One who is in charge of a ship." **Skip, Skipp, Skippy**

Slade (Old English) "From the valley." **Slayd**

Slate (Modern U.S.) "Like the stone." Name taken from the vocabulary word.

Sloan (Irish Gaelic) "A warrior." **Sloane**

Smith (Old English) "A blacksmith." **Smitty, Smythe**

Solomon (Hebrew) Biblical name meaning "peaceful one." In the Bible, Solomon was the king of Israel known for his extraordinary wisdom. **Salomon, Shalom, Shlomo, Sholem, Sol, Sollie, Solly, Zalman, Zollie, Zolly**

Somerset (Old English) "From the summer estate." W. Somerset Maugham, novelist. **Somers**

Sorley (Scandinavian) "Summer traveler." **Somerled**

Spark (Middle English) "Happy, gallant one." **Sparke, Sparkie, Sparky**

Spaulding (Old English) "From the divided meadow." Spalding Gray, actor. **Spalding**

Spencer (Middle English) "One who dispenses supplies or provisions." Spencer Christian, TV journalist; Spencer Tracy, actor. **Spence, Spense, Spenser**

Spike (English) Usually a nickname referring to "an unruly tuft of hair." Spike Lee, movie writer, director, and producer.

Spiridon (Greek) "Full of soul or of the spirit." Spiro Agnew, thirty-ninth U.S. vice president. **Spire, Spiridion, Spiro, Spyro**

Sprague (Old French) "Lively one."

Stacey (Latin) "Stable, established one." Stacy Keach, actor. **Stace, Stacy**

Stafford (Old English) "From the landing place in the river." **Staffard, Staford**

Stamford (Old English) "From the stony river crossing." **Ford, Stan, Standford, Stanford.**

Stanhope (Old English) "From the stony hollow." **Stan**

Stanislaus (Polish) "In a glorious position." St. Stanislaus, patron saint of Poland. **Stan, Stanislav, Stanislaw**

Stanley (Old English) "From the meadow of stones." Stanley Kubrick, film director. **Stan, Stanleigh, Stanton**

Stanton (Middle English) "From the stone estate."

Stanwick (Old English) "From the village full of stones." **Stan, Stanway, Stanwood, Wick**

Stein (German) "Stonelike." **Steinn, Sten**

Stearne (Middle English) "Austere one." **Stearn, Stern**

Stephen (Greek) Biblical name meaning "crowned one." Name of the first Christian martyr. Steve McQueen and Steve Hanks, actors; Steve Allen, entertainer; Stephen King, writer; Stephen Spielberg, film director and producer. **Étienne, Staffan, Stefan, Stefano, Steffen, Stephan, Steve, Steven, Stevie**

Sterling (Middle English) "A little star." Sterling Hayden, actor. **Stirling**

Stewart (Old English) "A keeper of the estate." **Stew, Steward, Stu, Stuart**

Stian (Scandinavian) "Wanderer." **Stig, Stigand**

Stillman (Old English) "Quiet man." **Stillmann**

Stoddard (Old English) "One who keeps horses."

Storm (English) "Like a tempest."

Stowe (Old English) "Of the place."

Stratton (Old English) "From the town by the river." **Stratt, Stratford**

Stuart (Old English) Form of Stewart.

Suffield (Old English) "From the south field." **Suffie, Suffy**

Sullivan (Irish Gaelic) "Hawk-eyed one." **Sullie, Sully, Van**

Sumner (Middle English) "One who summons."

Sutherland (Scandinavian) "From the southern land." **Sutherlan**

Sutton (Old English) "From the town in the South."

Sven (Scandinavian) "A youth or young man." **Svein, Svend, Swen**

Swain (Middle English) "A young herdsman." **Swaine, Swane, Swayne, Wain**

Sweeney (Irish Gaelic) "Small hero."

■ NAMES HAVE MEANING ■

Naming experts agree that names affect a person's self-image. With this in mind, it is hard to imagine choosing a name for your child with any negative connotations. Even if Judas is the name of your favorite relative, others will undoubtedly think of a traitor. There are reasons that Hedda, Jezebel, Ebenezer, and Tristam have never appeared on popular name charts.

While choosing a positive-image name such as Victoria or Alexander doesn't ensure that your child will be victorious or help mankind, it does provide a positive framework. Make sure the name you choose conveys to your child the meaning you want him or her to receive and to carry throughout life.

BOYS
T

Tab (Middle English) "A drummer." Tab Hunter, actor. **Tabby**

Tad (Irish Gaelic) "A philosopher." Form of Tadhg or Thaddeus. **Tadd**

Tadhg (Irish Gaelic) "A poet or philospher." **Taogh, Teague, Teigue**

Talbot (Old French) "One who pillages." (Old English) "Like a talbot," referring to an extinct dog similar to a bloodhound. **Talbert, Tally**

Tammaro (Old German) "A famous thinker." **Tammare**

Tanner (Old English) "One who works with leather." **Tan, Tanney, Tannie, Tanny**

Tate (English) "Cheerful one." **Tait, Taite**

Taylor (Middle English) "A tailor." **Tailor**

Ted (Old English) Form of Edward and Theodore. Ted Koppel, broadcast journalist; Ted Turner, founder of CNN; Ted Williams, baseball player. **Tedd, Teddy, Tedman, Tedmund**

Templeton (Old English) "From the town with a temple." The name was sometimes used for children who were left at the temple door. **Temp, Temple**

Tennessee (American) U.S. state name used as a first name. Tennessee Williams, playwright. **Tenny**

Terence (Latin) "Gentle and smooth." (Irish Gaelic) "An instigator." **Tarrance, Terencio, Terrance, Terrence, Terry**

Tertius (Latin) "Third son." **Tertus**

Thaddeus (Greek) "Given by God." (Hebrew) "Praised one." **Tad, Thad, Thaddie, Thady**

Thatcher (Old English) "A roof thatcher." **Thacher, Thackeray, Thatch, Thaxter**

Thayer (Old German-English) "Of the national army."

Theobald (Old German) "Having the power of the people." **Ted, Teddy, Theo, Thibaud, Thibold, Tiebold, Tybalt**

Theodore (Greek) "God's gift." Theodore Roosevelt, twenty-sixth U.S. president; Theodore Dreiser, novelist; Dr. Theodor Seuss Geisel, author of children's books. **Feodor, Teador, Ted, Tedd, Teddie, Teddy, Teodor, Theo, Theodor, Theodore**

Theodoric (Old German) "All-powerful ruler." **Derek, Dietrich, Dirk, Ted, Teodorico, Thedric, Thedrick, Thierry**

Theron (Greek) "A hunter."

Thomas (Hebrew) Biblical name meaning "a twin." Thomas was one of the twelve Apostles. Tom Brokaw, broadcast journalist; Thomas Jefferson, third U.S. president; Thomas Edison, inventor; Thomas Mann, German novelist; Tom Selleck, actor; Tom Wolfe, American novelist. **Tam, Thom, Tom, Tomag, Tomas, Tomaso, Tommaso, Tommie, Tommy, Tomos**

Thor (Scandinavian) "Of the thunder." **Thorvald, Tor, Torin**

Thorndike (Old English) "From the thorny dike." **Thorndyke, Thornie, Thorny**

Thornley (Old English) "From the thorn-covered meadow." **Thorne**

Thornton (Old English) "From the town or estate full of thorns." Thornton Wilder, writer. **Thorn, Thorndike, Thornie, Thorny**

Thorpe (Old English) "From the small village."

Thurston (Scandinavian) "Thor's jeweled stone." Thurston Howell III, character on the TV show *Gilligan's Island*. **Thorstein, Thorsten, Thurstan**

Tiernan (Irish Gaelic) "Lordly." **Tierney**

Timothy (Greek) Biblical name meaning "one who honors God." Timothy Hutton, actor; Timothy Leary, psychologist known for experimenting with hallucinogenic drugs. **Tim, Timmie, Timmy, Timoteo, Timothee, Tymothy**

Tirion (Welsh) "Kind, gentle one."

Titus (Greek) "From the giants." In classical Greek mythology, Titus is the giant slain by Apollo. **Tite, Tito, Titos, Tiziano, Tytus**

Tobias (Hebrew) Biblical name meaning "from the goodness of God." **Tobe, Tobi, Tobiah, Tobie, Toby**

Todd (Middle English) "Foxlike." Todd Rundgren, pop musician.

Toland (Old English) "One inhabiting the taxed land." **Tolle**

Tomkin (Old English) "A small Tom." **Tomlin**

Tony (English) "Priceless one." Form of Anthony. Tony Bennett, singer; Tony Randall, actor. **Toni, Tonio**

Torger (Scandinavian) "Thunderous warrior." **Terje, Torgeir**

Torrance (Irish Gaelic) "From the sea full of small hills or knolls." **Tore, Torey, Torin, Torrence, Torrey, Torrin**

Townsend (Old English) "From the end of town." **Town, Townie, Towny**

Travis (Old French) "One who makes a crossing or is at the crossroads." **Travers, Travus**

Tremain (Celtic) "From the rocky settlement." **Tremaine, Tremayne**

Trent (Latin) "Torrent."

Trevor (Irish Gaelic) "From the large estate." Trevor Howard, actor; Trevor Nunn, director. **Trefor, Trev, Trevar, Trever**

Tristan (Welsh) "Sad or sorrowful one." Hero of the romantic legend Tristan and Isolde. Tristan Tzara, French poet responsible for founding the Dada movement. **Tristam, Tristram, Trystan**

Troy (Irish Gaelic) "A young foot soldier." (Old French) "Curly-haired one." Troy Donahue, actor. **Troi**

Truman (Old English) "One who is trustworthy." Truman Capote, writer. **Trueman, Trumann**

Trumble (Old English) "Brave, strong one." **Trumball**

Tucker (Old English) "One who tucks cloth." **Tuck**

Tully (Irish Gaelic) "Devoted to the peace of God." **Tull, Tulley**

Turner (Latin) "Lathe worker; one who turns wood."

Tycho (Greek) "One who hits the mark." Tycho Brahe, Danish astronomer. **Tyge, Tyko**

Tyler (Old English) "Tile- or brickmaker." **Tiler, Ty, Tye**

Tynan (Irish Gaelic) "Dark one."

Tyrone (Greek) "A king or ruler." Tyrone Power, actor. **Ty, Tyron**

BOYS
U

Uan (Irish Gaelic) "Lamblike."

Udell (Old English) "From the valley of yew trees." **Udale, Udall**

Ugo (Italian) "Intelligent one." Form of Hugh. **Hugo**

Ulf (Swedish) "Wolflike one." **Ulfred, Ulv**

Ulrich (Old German) "Having a powerful fortune or large estate." The name of two German saints. **Oldrich, Ulrik, Ulryk, Utz**

Ulysses (Latin) "Angry one." Form of the Greek name Odysseus. Ulysses S. Grant, eighteenth U.S. president. **Ulises, Ulisses**

Upton (Old English) "From the upper town." Upton Sinclair, author.

Urban (Latin) "Of the big city." **Orban, Urbain, Urbaine, Urbano, Urvan**

Uriah (Hebrew) Biblical name meaning "the light is my God." Uriah Heep, character in Charles Dickens's *David Copperfield*. **Uri, Uria, Urias, Urie**

Uriel (Hebrew) Biblical name meaning "God is my light." A more common modern form of Uriah. **Uri, Yuri**

Urs (Latin) "Bearlike." **Urson**

Uzziel (Hebrew) Biblical name meaning "one with the power of God." **Uzi, Uziel, Uzziah**

BOYS
V

Vaast (Old German) "A visitor to the woods." **Vedast, Vedastus**

Vachel (Old French) "One who keeps cows." Vachel Lindsay, poet.

Vail (Old English) "Of the valley." **Vale**

Valdemar (Old German) "Renowned ruler." **Valdis**

Valentine (Latin) "Strong one." St. Valentine, famous Roman martyr. **Val, Valentin, Valentino**

Van (Dutch) "Of or from." Prefix to many Dutch names. Van Johnson, actor; Van Morrison, pop singer.

Vance (Latin) "One who stays ahead." (Old English) "From near the marsh." **Van**

Vasilis (Greek) "Royal, magnificent one." **Vasos**

Vassily (Russian) "Definitive guardian." **Vas, Vassi**

Vaughn (Welsh) "Little one." Vaughn Monroe, singer. **Vaughan**

Vernon (Latin) "Of the springtime." Vernon Duke, composer. **Verne, Verner, Verney**

Verrill (Old French) "True one." **Verrall, Verrell, Veryl**

Victor (Latin) "Victorious." Victor Borge, singer and comedian. **Vic, Vick, Vittorio**

Vidal (Latin) "Life." Vidal Sassoon, British hairstylist.

Vincent (Latin) "Conqueror." Vincente Minnelli, movie director; Vincent Van Gogh, artist. **Vin, Vince, Vincente, Vinny, Vinson**

Vine (English) "One who works in a vineyard."

Virgil (Latin) "He who carries the staff of authority." **Verge, Vergil**

Vitus (Latin) "Live one." Vitas Gerulaitis, tennis player. **Vit, Vitas, Vite, Vito, Wit, Witold**

Vladimir (Russian) "Ruling in peace." Vladimir Nabokov, writer.

■ THE QUESTION OF GENDER ■

Unisex names are becoming increasingly popular. This trend began in the 1960s, when parents rebelled against traditional male or female names. The feeling was that gender-specific names only worked to further the sexual stereotyping already prevalent in our society.

Today, unisex names have moved from the cutesy ones of the 1960s (Jamie, Jody, and Nicky) to the conservative names of the 1990s (Avery, Carter, and Taylor).

If you decide on a unisex name for your child, keep in mind that girls have an easier time living with masculine names than boys have with feminine ones. Here are some names that a son might have trouble coping with:

Alexis	Laurie/Loren
Ashley	Leslie
Carey	Lindsey
Carroll	Meredith
Darcy	Merle
Gale	Robin
Jody	Sydney
Kelly	Terry

BOYS
W

Wade (Old English) "From the place where it's shallow enough to wade across the river." **Wadley, Wadsworth**

Wainwright (Old English) "Builder of wagons." **Wagner, Wain, Waine, Wayne, Wright**

Waite (Middle English) "A watchman."

Wakefield (Old English) "Of the flooded fields." **Field, Waike, Wake, Wakeley**

Walby (Old English) "From the walled-in estate." **Walbie**

Walcott (Old English) "From the walled-in cottage." **Walcot**

Waldemar (Old German) "Famous ruler." **Valdemar, Vladimir, Waldo**

Walden (Old English) "Of the woods." Title of book by Henry David Thoreau. **Waldon**

Waldo (Old German) "Powerful ruler." Form of Waldemar. Ralph Waldo Emerson, writer and philosopher.

Walker (Old English) "One who cleans cloth," referring to a process of walking on the cloth to cleanse it.

Wallace (Old English) "From Wales." Wallace Shawn, actor. **Wallie, Wallis, Wally, Walsh, Welch, Welsh**

Waller (Old English) "One who builds walls." (Old German) "Army leader." **Wallor**

Walt Form of Walter and Walton. Walt Whitman, poet; Walt Disney, movie producer.

Walter (Old German) "Ruler of the people." Walter Brennan and Walter Matthau, actors; Walter Cronkite, TV journalist; Walter Mondale, forty-second U.S. vice president. **Gauther, Gutierre, Valter, Wallie, Wally, Walt, Waltr**

Walton (Old English) "From the walled town." **Wallie, Wally, Walt**

Ward (Old English) "Guardian or watchman." **Warde, Warden**

Warren (Old English) "Keeper of a game preserve." (Old

German) "Protector." Warren Harding, twenty-ninth president; Warren Beatty, actor. **Ware, Waring**

Warwick (Old English) "From the farm or estate near a weir." (Old German) "A strong ruler." **Warick, Warley, Warrick**

Washington (Old English) "From the town of the wise one." The name now honors George Washington, the first U.S. president; Washington Irving, writer. **Wash**

Watson (Old English) "Son of Walter." **Wat, Watkin, Wattie, Watty**

Wayland (Old English) "Of the land by the roadway." Waylon Jennings, country and western singer. **Way, Waylan, Waylen, Waylon, Weylan, Weylin**

Wayne (Old English) "One who makes or drives wagons." Wayne Gretzky, ice hockey player; Wayne Newton, singer. **Wain, Waine, Wayn**

Webster (Old English) "A weaver." Webster Slaughter, football player. **Webb, Webber**

Weldon (Old English) "From the estate with a spring." **Welton**

Wellington (Old English) "From the estate of the prosperous one."

Wells (Old English) "From the spring."

Wencelas (Old Slavic) "One of great glory." The name of four kings of Bohemia as well as the patron saint of Bohemia. **Wencelaus, Wenzel, Wenzeslaus**

Wendell (Old German) "A wanderer." Oliver Wendell Holmes, justice of the U.S. Supreme Court; Wendell Willkie, U.S. political leader. **Wende, Wendel, Wendelin**

Wentworth (Old English) "From the white one's manor or estate."

Werner (Old German) "Protective warrior." Werner Erhardt, founder of EST. **Warner, Wernher**

Wesley (Old English) "From the western meadow." **Lee, Leigh, Wellesley, Wes, West, Westley**

Westbrook (Old English) "From the western brook."

Weston (Old English) "From the western town or estate." **Wes, West, Westcott**

Wharton (Old English) "From the town near the shore." **Whart, Wharty**

Whitmore (Old English) "From the whitish-colored moor."

Whitney (Old English) "From the island of the white-haired ones." **Whit**

Whittaker (Old English) "From the white field." **Whit, Whitaker**

Wickley (Old English) "From the enclosed meadow." **Wick, Wickham**

Wilbur (German) Form of Gilbert. Wilbur Wright, aviation pioneer. **Wilber, Wilberforce, Wilbert, Wilburt**

Wiley (Old English) "Charming one." **Wye, Wylie**

Wilfred (Old German) "Resolute and peaceful."

Willard (Old German) "One with a will of steel." Willard Scott, *The Today Show* host. **Will, Willie, Willy**

William (Old German) "A guardian with firm determination." William the Conqueror; William Shakespeare, William Styron and William Faulkner, writers; William Hurt and Willem Dafoe, actors; Willie Mays, baseball player; Willie Nelson, singer. **Bill, Billie, Billy, Guillaume, Liam, Wilhelm, Will, Willem, Willie, Willy, Wilmer, Uilleam, Vilem**

Willoughby (Old English) "From the settlement by the willow trees." **Will**

Wilson (Old English) "Son of William." Wilson Pickett, rock musician.

Wilton (Old English) "From the settlement near the spring." Wilt Chamberlain, basketball player. **Will, Wilt**

Wingate (Old English) "From near the winding or swinging gate." **Win**

Winslow (Old English) "From the friend's hillside." Winslow Homer, American artist.

Winston (Old English) "From the friend's town." Sir Winston Churchill, British prime minister.

Winthrop (Old English) "From the friend's village." **Winn, Wyn**

Witt (Old English) "Wise one." **Witter, Wittier**

Wolcott (Old English-German) "From the brave, wolflike one's cottage." **Wolcot**

Wolfgang (Old German) "Like a wolf advancing." Wolfgang Amadeus Mozart, composer. **Wolf, Wolfe, Wolfie, Wolfy**

Woodrow (Old English) "From the row of houses near the wood." Woody Allen, film director, writer, and actor; Woodrow Wilson, twenty-eighth U.S. president; Woody Guthrie, folk singer. **Wood, Woodie, Woody**

Woodward (Old English) "Protector of the woods." **Woodie, Woody, Ward**

Worth (Old English) "From the farm or homestead." **Worthington, Worthy**

Wright (Old English) "One who works with wood."

Wyatt (Old French) "Small warrior." **Wiatt, Wyat, Wye**

Wyman (Old English) "Warrior." **Wymer**

Wynn (Old Welsh) "Fair."

■ DON'T WORRY, ANYONE CAN CHANGE HIS OR HER NAME ■

Americans are known for changing their names. Certainly immigrants coming into the United States were encouraged, even forced, to take knew, more American-sounding names. While we think of movie stars as being mainly responsible for the popularity of name changing today, there are many people who take on new names for many different reasons. Their name may be too old-fashioned, too hard to pronounce, difficult to spell, carry negative associations, promote corny nicknames, be too effeminate (for men), or convey a religious belief or stereotype that isn't appropriate. Whatever the reason, everybody has a right in this country to change their name. Here are some famous names and the real ones behind them.

CHANGED TO	CHANGED FROM	POSSIBLE REASON
Gerald Ford	Leslie Lynch King, Jr.	Adoptive parents' name
Muhammad Ali	Cassius Marcellus Clay, Jr.	Religious
Woody Allen	Allen Konigsberg	Too foreign
Walter Matthau	Walter Matuschanskayasky	Too difficult to pronounce
Meryl Streep	Mary Louise Streep	Too old-fashioned
John Wayne	Marion Michael Morrison	Too effeminate
Stevie Wonder	Steveland Morris Hardaway	Nickname that stuck
Eric Clapton	Eric Clap	Promotes corny nicknames
Lee Grant	Lyova Haskell Rosenthal	Too forgettable
Mike Nichols	Michael Igor Peschkowsky	Too foreign

Boys XYZ

Xavier (Spanish) "Owner of the new household." Xavier McDaniel, basketball player. **Javier, Saverio, Zavier**

Xenos (Greek) "Newcomer or stranger." **Xenophon**

Xerxes (Persian) "Ruling king." Name of a famous ancient Persian king. **Zerk**

Xylon (Greek) "Of the forest."

Yakov (Modern Hebrew) "A supplanter." Form of Jacob. **Yaakov, Yasha**

Yale (Old English) "From the fertile land on the hill." A name that is mainly associated with Yale University. **Yaley, Yalie**

Yancy (American Indian) "An Englishman or Yankee." **Yance, Yank, Yankee**

Yardley (Old English) "From the fenced clearing." **Lee, Leigh, Yard**

Yasir (Arabic) "Wealthy one for whom things come easily." Yasir Arafat, Palestinian political leader. **Yasah, Yasser, Yusra, Yusri**

Yates (Old English) "From the gates of the enclosed settlement." **Yeates**

Yefim (Greek) "One who speaks well."

Yegor (Russian) Form of George.

Yehudi (Hebrew) "Praised one." **Judah**

York (Old English) "From the boar farm." **Yorke, Yorker**

Yosef (Modern Hebrew) Form of Joseph.

Yule (Old English) "One born at Yuletide or Christmastime." Yul Brynner, actor. **Yuell, Yul**

Yuri (Russian) Form of George. Yuri Andropov, Soviet political leader. **Juri**

Yves (French) "A small archer." St. Yves, patron saint of lawyers. Yves Montand, French actor; Yves St. Laurent, fashion designer. **Ives, Ivo, Ivor**

Zachary (Hebrew) Biblical name meaning "one remembered by God." Form of Zachariah. Zachariah was the father of John the Baptist. Zachary Taylor, twelfth U.S. president. **Zacarias, Zaccaroa, Zach, Zachariah, Zacharie, Zack, Zackie, Zacky, Zak, Zechariah, Zeke**

Zalman (Yiddish) "One of peace." Form of Soloman.

Zared (Hebrew) "Ambush."

Zarek (Greek) "God protects our king."

Zayd (Arabic) "To become greater." **Zaid**

Zebadiah (Hebrew) Biblical name meaning "one whom God believes." **Zebedee**

Zebulon (Hebrew) Biblical name meaning "to live with." Zebulon was the sixth son of Jacob and Leah. **Zabulon, Zeb**

Zedekiah (Hebrew) Biblical name meaning "from the justice of God." **Zed**

Zelig (Hebrew) "Happy, fortunate one." **Selig**

Zenas (Greek) "Living one" or "given life by Zeus." **Zenon, Zenos**

Zephaniah (Hebrew) Biblical name meaning "one hidden by God." **Zeph, Zephan**

Zeus (Greek) "Great father of all." In Greek mythology, Zeus was the ruler of heaven and the father of gods and men.

Zimri (Hebrew) Biblical name meaning "one celebrated in song."

Zolly (Hebrew) Form of Saul and Soloman. **Zol, Zollie**

Zvi (Hebrew) "Deerlike." **Zwi**

GIRLS

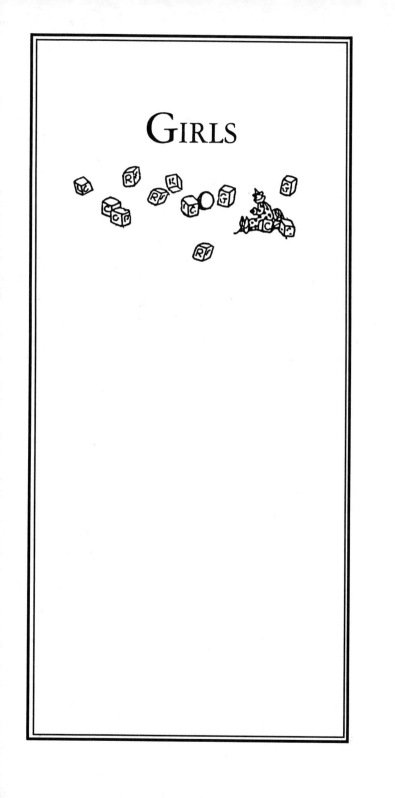

GIRLS
A

Abigail (Hebrew) Biblical name meaning "a source of great joy." Abigail Adams, wife of second U.S. president; Abigail Van Buren, newspaper columnist responsible for the *Dear Abby* column. **Abagael, Abagail, Abagale, Abbe, Abbey, Abbi, Abbie, Abby, Abbye, Abigael, Gael, Gail, Gale, Gayel**

Abilene (Hebrew) "From the grass-covered place." **Abbie.**

Abra (Hebrew) "Mother of many nations." Feminine form of Abraham. **Abira, Avra**

Acacia (Greek) "Thorny like the tree." The acacia tree symbolizes immortality and rebirth. **Cacia, Cacie, Casey, Casia, Kacie**

Ada (Old German) "Prosperous one." (Hebrew) "An ornament." **Adah, Addia, Addie, Adda, Adey, Adi, Aida, Eada, Eda**

Adamina (Latin) "Woman of the earth." Feminine form of Adam. **Ada, Addie, Mina**

Adara (Greek) "Beautiful one." (Arabic) "Virginal one." **Ada**

Adelaide (Old German) "Of noble birth." Adelaide was the wife of King William IV of England. Adele Simpson, fashion designer. **Addi, Addie, Adela, Adele, Adelheid, Adelia, Adelina, Adeline, Adella, Aleida, Della, Edeline, Heidi**

Adena (Hebrew) "Sensuous or desirable one." **Adina, Adine, Dena, Dina**

Adrienne (Latin) "Dark, beautiful one." Adrienne Rich, U.S. poet. **Adrea, Adria, Adriana, Adriane, Adrianne, Adriene, Hadra**

Africa (English) The place name used as a first name. **Affrica, Africah, Afrika**

Agatha (Greek) "Kind, good one." Agatha Christie, mystery writer. **Ag, Agace, Agathe, Aggi, Aggie, Aggy**

Agnes (Greek) "Pure, virginal one." Agnes Moorhead, actress; Agnes De Mille, choreographer. **Aggie, Agna, Agnese, Agneta, Agnethe, Annis, Ina, Ines, Inessa, Inez, Nessa, Nessi, Nessie, Nessy, Nesta, Nevsa, Una, Ynes, Ynez**

Aidan (Irish Gaelic) "Little fiery one" or "one full of warmth." **Aden, Aiden, Edan**

Aileen (Irish) "One who brightens the spirit." Form of Helen. **Aila, Ailee, Ailene, Ailey, Alanna, Alayne, Allene, Eileen, Ileana, Ileane, Ilene, Lana, Lena, Lina**

Ainslie (Scottish Gaelic) "Of one's own meadow." **Ainslee, Ainsley, Ansley**

Aisha (Arabic) "Of life." **Asha, Ashia, Asia**

Alameda (Spanish) "Poplar tree."

Alanna (Irish Gaelic) "Beautiful, harmonious one." Feminine form of Allan. **Alaine, Alana, Alane, Alannah, Alayna, Alleen, Allene, Allina, Allyn, Lana, Lanna**

Alberta (Old English) "Bright, noble one." Feminine form of Albert. **Alba, Albertina, Albertine, Alby, Ali, Alverta, Auberta, Aubine, Bert, Berta, Bertie, Berty, Elberta, Elbertina, Elbertine**

Alcina (Greek) "Strong minded." **Alcine, Alcinia**

Alda (Old German) "Old and wise." Feminine form of Aldo. **Alida**

Alethea (Greek) "One who is true." **Aleta, Aletha, Alethia**

Alexandra (Greek) "Helper of mankind." Feminine form of Alexander. Princess Alexandra of Kent. **Alejandra, Alejandrina, Aleksandra, Alessandra, Alessia, Alexa, Alexandrina, Alexia, Alexina, Alexine, Alexis, Ali, Allie, Lesya, Lexi, Lexy, Sandra, Sandy, Sanya, Sasha, Sondra, Zandra**

Alfreda (Old English) "Wise counselor." Feminine form of Alfred. **Alfie, Elfreda, Elfrida, Elfrieda, Elva, Freda**

Alice (Greek) "One who is true." (Old German) "Of noble descent." Name of the main character in Lewis Carroll's *Alice in Wonderland*. Alice Walker, American writer; Ali McGraw, actress. **Adelice, Ailis, Alecia, Aleece, Ali, Alicia, Alisha, Alissa, Allie, Allys, Alyce, Alys, Alyssa, Elissa, Elsie, Ilysa, Ilyssa, Lissa, Lyssa**

Alida (Greek) "Beautifully dressed." **Aleda, Aletta, Allida, Lida**

Aline (Irish Gaelic) "Lovely, illustrious one." **Alina, Aleine, Alene, Alyna**

Alison (Irish Gaelic) "True one." Form of Alice. Ally Sheedy, actress. **Ali, Alli, Allison, Ally, Allyson, Alyson, Alyssa, Lissi, Lissie, Lissy**

Aliza (Hebrew) "Joyous one." **Alisa, Alyssa**

Allegra (Italian) "Lively, joyful one." A musical term used as a name. **Allie, Legra**

Alma (Latin) "Nurturing one." Alma mater, term often used for an educational establishment meaning "fostering mother."

Almeda (Latin) "Pressing toward the goal." **Almeta**

Almira (Arabic) "Princess or lofty one." **Elmira**

Alpha (Greek) "Firstborn." **Alfa**

Althea (Greek) "A healer" or "wholesome one." Althea Gibson, tennis player. **Elthea, Thea**

Alva (Latin) "White-haired or -skinned." Feminine form of Alvin. **Alvah, Alvita**

Alvina (Old English) "A noble and true friend." **Alvinia, Vina, Vinnie, Vinny**

Amabel (Latin) "Lovable." **Amabelle, Belle**

Amanda (Latin) "One fit to be loved." Amanda Plummer, actress. **Amandine, Amata, Manda, Mande, Mandie, Mandy**

Amara (Greek) "Of eternal beauty." **Amargo, Margo**

Amaris (Hebrew) "Promised by God." **Amariah, Amaryah**

Amaryllis (Greek) "Sparkling one."

Amber (Arabic) "Jewel-like one." Name of the heroine in Kathleen Winsor's novel *Forever Amber*. **Amberly, Ambur**

Amelia (Latin) "Industrious one." Name of the heroine in Henry Fielding's novel *Amelia*. Amelia Earhart, first woman in flight. **Amalea, Amalee, Amalia, Amalie, Ameline, Amie, Amy, Emelie, Emilia**

Amethyst (Greek) "Jewel-like or wine-colored." Name given after the birthstone for February.

Amity (French) "Of friendship." **Amice, Amita, Amitie**

Amy (French) "One well loved." Amy Irving, actress; Amy Lowell, poet; Amy Vanderbilt, authority on etiquette. **Aimee, Amata, Ame, Ami, Amie, Amey, Esma, Esme**

Anastasia (Greek) "One who is resurrected." Name of one of the daughters of the Russian czar Nicholas II. **Ana, Anastasie, Anastassia, Ann, Anna, Anne, Annie, Asia, Asya, Stacey, Stacie, Stacy**

Anatola (Greek) "From the East." **Anatolia**

Andrea (Greek) "Womanly one." Feminine form of Andrew. Andie MacDowell, actress. **Andi, Andie, Andreana, Andree, Andria, Andriana, Andrina, Andrine, Andy**

Angela (Greek) "Angel or messenger from heaven." Angela Lansbury, Angie Dickinson, actresses. **Angel, Angele, Angelina, Angelita, Angie, Angy, Gelya**

Angelica (Latin) "Angel-like." Anjelica Huston, actress. **Angelika, Angelique, Anjelica**

Aniella (Italian) "Lamblike" **Aniela**

Anita (Spanish) Form of Ann. Anita Bryant, singer, social activist, and promoter of Florida orange juice; Anita Hill, law professor. **Anitra**

Ann (Hebrew) Biblical name meaning "one full of grace." Anna is the name of the mother of the Virgin Mary. Anne Bancroft, actress; Anaïs Nin and Ayn Rand, novelist. **Aine, Ana, Anais, Anette, Ania, Anica, Anita, Anitra, Anna, Annah, Anne, Annie, Annika, Annina, Anny, Anouska, Anushka, Anya, Ayn, Nan, Nana, Nancee, Nancey, Nanci, Nancie, Nancy, Nanette, Nannie, Nanny, Nina, Ninette, Nita**

Annabel (Latin) "Lovable one." Or Anna and Belle meaning "beautiful, graceful one." **Anabel, Anabella, Anabelle, Annabell, Annabella, Annabelle**

Annette (English) Diminutive form of Ann. Annette Bening, actress. **Anet, Anett, Anetta, Ann, Anne, Netta, Nettie, Netty**

Anona (Latin) "Of the crops." **Annona**

Antigone (Greek) "Born contrary to custom." In classical Greek mythology, Antigone was the daughter of Oedipus by his accidental marriage to his own mother.

Antonia (Latin) "Priceless one." Feminine form of Anthony. Antonia Fraser, English writer. **Antinette, Antoinette, Antonetta, Antonie, Antonietta, Netta, Nettie, Netty, Toni, Tonia, Tonie, Tony**

April (Latin) "One who is opening up or blooming," referring to the month when the earth opens for spring's growth. **Aprilette, Averil, Averyl, Avril**

Arabella (Latin) "Full of the beauty of prayer." **Ara, Arabela, Arabelle, Bel, Bella, Belle, Bellie**

Ardelle (Latin) "Enthusiastic, fervent one." **Arda, Ardeen, Ardelia, Ardelis, Ardella, Ardene, Ardent, Ardine, Ardis, Ardra**

Arden (Old English) "From the valley of eagles." **Ardeen, Ardenia**

Ardith (Hebrew) "Flowering field." **Ardath, Ardyce, Ardys, Ardyth, Datha**

Aretha (Greek) "Virtuous, good one." Aretha Franklin, singer. **Aretta, Oretha, Retha**

Aria (Italian) "Melodious one." **Arietta, Ariette**

Ariadne (Greek) "Holy one." In classical Greek mythology, Ariadne is the daughter of the Cretan king Minos. **Ariana, Arianna, Arianne**

Ariel (Hebrew) "Lionesslike" or "strong like God." The name of the main character in Walt Disney's movie *The Little Mermaid*. **Aeriel, Ariela, Ariella, Arielle**

Arlene (Irish Gaelic) "Pledged one." Arlene Francis, actress. **Arelyn, Arlana, Arlee, Arleen, Arlen, Arlena, Arlie, Arliene, Arlina, Arlinda, Arline, Arlyne, Lena, Lina**

Ashley (Old English) "Of the ash-tree meadow." **Ash, Ashlea, Ashleigh, Ashlen, Ashly**

Asta (Greek) "Starlike" **Astera, Astra, Astrea, Asteroa, Estella, Stella**

Astrid (Scandinavian) "As beautiful as a goddess" and "as strong as a god." Name of a Belgian queen. **Asta, Astra, Estrid, Sassa, Sassy**

Atalanta (Greek) "Mighty, unswaying one." American place name. **Atlanta, Altante**

Atalaya (Spanish) "Protector."

Atara (Hebrew) Biblical name meaning "crownlike." **Atarah, Atera**

Athena (Greek) "One who is wise." In classical Greek mythology, Athena is the goddess of wisdom, literally born out of the head of Zeus. **Athen, Athene, Athenia, Athie**

Audrey (Old English) "Of noble birth" or "strong one." Audrey Hepburn, actress. **Audre, Audria, Audrie, Audry, Audrye**

Augusta (Latin) "Magnificent, venerable one." Feminine form of Augustus. **Augustina, Augustine, Gussie, Tina**

Aurelia (Latin) "Golden-haired" or "golden one." The name in Roman mythology of the goddess of the dawn. **Aura, Aurea, Aurel, Aurelie, Auria, Aurie, Aurora, Oralee, Orelia, Rory**

Autumn (Latin) "Autumn." The season used as a name.

Avery (Old English) "Small but wise counselor."

Avita (Latin) "Birdlike. "Ava Gardner, actress. **Ava, Avice, Avis, Avisa**

Azalea (Latin) "Of the dry earth." The azalea flower grows even in very dry earth.

Azelia (Hebrew) "One whom God helps." **Azel, Azela, Aziel**

Aviva (Modern Hebrew) "Springlike" or "born in the spring."
Avivah, Avrit, Viva

Azucena (Spanish) "Like the madonna lily," referring to the white purity of the Virgin Mary.

Azura (Persian) "Like the blue sky." **Azur**

GIRLS
B

Bambi (Italian) "Baby" or "child." Short for *bambino*. **Bambie, Bamby**

Barbara (Latin) "One who is strange or foreign," originally referring to the unintelligible babble of foreigners. St. Barbara is the patron saint of architects. Barbara Hershey and Barbra Streisand, actresses; Barbara Walters, TV journalist. **Bab, Babby, Babette, Babs, Barb, Barbe, Barbette, Barbi, Barbra, Barby, Basia, Bobbee, Bobbi, Bobbie, Bobby, Varina**

Basilia (Greek) "Regal one." Feminine form of Basil. **Basile**

Bathsheba (Hebrew) Biblical name meaning "daughter of the oath." The beautiful Bathsheba became the wife of King David in the Bible. The more common form used today is Sheba. **Bathia, Batsheva, Sheba, Sheva**

Beatrice (Latin) "One who brings joy." Beatrix Potter, English author of children's stories; Beatrice Arthur, actress. **Bea, Beata, Beatrisa, Beatrix, Beatrys, Beattie, Bebe, Bee, Beitris, Trix, Trixie, Trixy**

Becky (English) Form of Rebecca. **Beca, Becca**

Belinda (Old Spanish) "Beautiful one." (Modern German) "One with the cunning of a serpent." **Belle, Belynda, Linda, Lyn, Lynn**

Belle (French) "One who is beautiful." (Czech) "White one." Bella Abzug, feminist and U.S. politician; name of the protagonist in the Walt Disney movie *Beauty and the Beast*. **Bel, Bell, Bella, Belvia, Bill, Billie**

Benita (Latin) "Blessed one." **Benedetta, Benedicata, Benetta, Benni, Bennie, Benny, Benoite, Bin, Binny**

Bernadette (French) "Brave one." Feminine form of Bernard. Bette Midler and Bernadette Peters, singers and

■ How Many Meanings in a Name ■

You might want to double-check the dictionary after choosing the perfect name. Although I've listed the most common definitions, some unusual ones might surprise you, or even make you think twice. Your adorable little Jezebel may one day learn that her name is synonymous with women of low moral fiber. Here are a few examples of names that have become vocabulary words in their own right:

Bobby. Popular name in England for a London policeman. The name comes from Sir Robert Peel (1799–1850), who was responsible for the formation of London's metropolitan police in 1828.

Cain. An uproar or disturbance, as in "raising cain," named for the biblical Cain, who in a fit of jealousy murdered his brother Abel.

Cassandra. A person who predicts misfortune or disaster. In Greek mythology, Cassandra is the prophetic daughter of King Priam who foretells the fall of Troy but whom nobody believes.

Derrick. A derrick is a type of hoisting apparatus upon which a tackle is rigged. It is named for a famous seventeenth-century hangman who devised his own special equipment for executions.

Don Juan. An unscrupulous woman-chaser is named for the hero in a seventeenth-century Spanish play by Tirso de Molina. Don Juan Tenorio, a dissolute Spanish nobleman, murders the father of one of his female victims and receives his due when the father comes back to life. The idea of this character intrigued Byron, who wrote a satirical poem titled *Don Juan,* and Mozart, whose opera *Don Giovanni* recounts the legend.

Goliath. An extremely large person. The name comes from the biblical giant Goliath, who was stoned down by the young shepherd David.

Jezebel. An imprudent, shameless woman. The biblical Jezebel was a Phoenician princess who was given in marriage to King Ahab of Judah (875 B.C.) in an attempt to join the warring states of Judah and Phoenicia. A beautiful woman, Jezebel so captivated her husband that she was allowed to do as she pleased. The authors of the biblical Book of Kings describe her as "a merciless dictator, a wily intriguer, and a shameless trollop who paints her face."

John. A toilet. It appears that "a john" was named for an Englishman, Sir John Harrington, who claims to have invented a primitive flushing mechanism during the reign of Queen Elizabeth I.

Judas. A traitor. The name comes from the biblical Judas, who betrayed Christ.

Pollyanna. An unrealistically upbeat, optimistic person. The phrase is coined from the annoyingly cheerful heroine in Eleanor Hodgman Porter's novel *Polly-anna,* published in 1913. Living by what she calls the "glad game," Pollyanna finds the good in even the most dismal of circumstances.

Romeo. An extremely romantic male lover named for the hero in Shakespeare's romantic tragedy *Romeo and Juliet.*

---

actresses. **Berna, Bernadina, Bernadine, Bernardine, Bernetta, Bernita, Bernie, Berny, Bette**

Bernice (Greek) "One who brings victory." **Berenice, Bernelle, Bernie, Berny, Bunnie, Bunny, Nixie, Veronica, Veronique**

Bertha (Old German) "Bright, glorious one." **Berta, Berthe, Bertie, Bertina, Bertine, Berty, Bird**

Beryl (Greek) "A jewel." A sea-green color jewel of the emerald variety. Beryl Bainbridge, Enlish author.

Bessie (English) "One who believes God is perfection." Short form of Elizabeth. **Bess, Bessy**

Bethany (Hebrew) Biblical name probably meaning "from the house of God." In the New Testament it is the name of a town just outside Jerusalem where Jesus stayed before his Crucifixion. **Beth, Bethel, Bethena, Bethia, Bethina**

Betsy (English) Short form of Elizabeth. Betsy Ross, maker of the first American flag. **Bets, Betsie, Bettsie**

Betty (English) Short form of Elizabeth. Betty Ford, wife of thirty-eighth U.S. president; Betty Friedan, feminist writer; Bette Davis and Betty Grable, actresses. **Bette, Bettie, Bettina**

Beulah (Hebrew) "Married one." In the Bible, it is a place name for the land of Israel, and the connotation is the "heavenly" land. **Beula**

Beverly (Old English) "From the meadow inhabited by beavers." Beverly Sills, singer. **Bev, Beverlee, Beverley, Bevvy, Buffy, Verlie**

Bevin (Irish Gaelic) "Melodious one." **Beyvn**

Bianca (Italian) Form of Blanche. Bianca Jagger, socialite. **Bellanca, Blanca, Blanka**

Bibi (Arabic) "Lady."

Billie (Old English) "Resolute one." Billie Jean King, tennis player; Billie Holliday, singer. **Billi, Billy**

Bina (Hebrew) "Wise, understanding one." **Binah**

Blaine (Irish Gaelic) "Slender one." Blaine Trump, socialite. **Blane, Blayne**

Blair (Scottish Gaelic) "From the fields." Blair Brown, actress. **Blaire**

Blanche (Old French) "Fair, white one." **Blanch, Blinnie, Blinny**

Bliss (Old English) "Blissful one." **Blisse**

Blythe (Old English) "Joyous one." Blythe Danner, actress. **Blithe**

Bonita (Spanish) "Pretty one." Bo Derek, actress. **Bo, Bona, Bonie, Bony, Nita**

Bonnie (Scottish) "Good, attractive one." Bonnie Parker, famous bank robber accomplice (Bonnie and Clyde). **Bonnee, Bonni, Bonny, Bunnie, Bunny**

Brandy (Dutch) "A sweet liqueur." **Brandee, Brandi, Brandie**

Brenda (Scandinavian) "One with a flaming sword." Brenda Starr, comic strip character. **Bren, Brenn**

Brenna (Irish Gaelic) "Raven-haired." Feminine form of Brendon. **Brenn**

Brianna (Irish Gaelic) "Strong one." Feminine form of Brian. **Breana, Breanna, Breanne, Bria, Briana, Brianne, Brina, Bryan, Bryana, Bryn, Brynn**

Brett (Latin) "One who comes from Brittania." Name of the main character in Ernest Hemingway's novel *The Sun Also Rises*. **Bret**

Bridget (Irish Gaelic) "Strong one" or "one from on high." St. Bridget, patroness of Ireland. Brigitte Bardot, actress. **Beret, Berget, Biddie, Biddy, Birgit, Birgitta, Breeda, Bride, Brietta, Brigid, Brigida, Brigit, Brigitta, Brigitte, Brita**

Brittany (Latin) "From Great Britain." Britt Eckland, actress. **Brit, Britney, Britt, Britta, Britteny, Brittney**

Brooke (Old English) "From near the brook." Brooke Shields, actress. **Brook, Brooks**

Brunhilda (Old German) "Battle maiden." **Brunhilde, Hilda, Hilde, Hildy**

Buffy (English) Pet form of Elizabeth. Buffy Sainte-Marie, folksinger. **Buff, Buffie**

Bunny (English) "Like a baby rabbit." Often used as a pet form of Bernice or Bonnie. **Bunni, Bunnie**

GIRLS
C

Cadence (Latin) "Having rhythm." **Cadance, Cadena, Cadenza, Cadie, Cady**

Caitlin (Irish Gaelic) Form of Catherine. **Caitlan, Catlee, Catlin, Kaitlin, Kaitlyn, Kaitlynn**

Calandra (Greek) "Like a lark." **Cal, Calandre, Calley, Calli, Callie, Cally, Clandria**

Calida (Spanish) "Loving, warm one." **Calla, Callista**

Calista (Greek) "The most beautiful." **Calesta, Calysta**

Cameo (Italian) "A sculptured jewel."

Cameron (Scottish Gaelic) "One with a crooked nose." **Cammie, Cammy**

Camilla (Latin) Possibly "a helper at a religious ceremony." **Camila, Camile, Camille, Cammie, Cammy, Millie, Milly**

Campbell (Scottish Gaelic) "Crooked-mouthed one." Campbell McCoy, character in Tom Wolfe's *Bonfire of the Vanities*. **Cam, Cammie, Cammy**

Candace (Greek) "Iridescent white one." Name of many queens of ancient Ethiopia. Candice Bergen, actress. **Candi, Candice, Candis, Candie, Candy, Kandace**

Candida (Latin) "One who is pure white." Name of a play by George Bernard Shaw. **Candi, Candide, Candie, Candy**

Candra (Latin) "Luminescent."

Caprice (Italian) "Whimsical, unpredictable one." **Capri, Capriccio**

Cara (Latin) "Dear one." (Irish Gaelic) "Friend." **Carina, Carine, Carrie, Kara**

Caresse (French) "Well-loved one." **Caresa, Caressa, Charissa**

Carilla (Old German) "A strong woman." Feminine form of Charles. **Cari**

Carina (Latin) "Dear, small one." **Caren, Carin, Carine, Karen**

Carissa (Latin) Form of Cara and Carina. **Carita, Karisa, Karissa**

Carla (Old German) "A strong country woman." Feminine form of Carl. Carly Simon, singer and songwriter. **Carly, Karla**

Carling (Irish Gaelic) "Small champion." Carling Bassett, tennis player.

Carmel (Hebrew) "From the garden," perhaps referring to one who is fertile and beautiful. **Carma, Carmela, Carmelina, Carmelita, Carmie, Carmy, Lita, Melina**

Carmen (Latin) "One with song." Name of the tragic heroine of Bizet's opera *Carmen*. **Carmine, Carmita, Charmaine**

Carol (Latin) "Strong and womanly." (French) "Joyous song," referring to Christmas carols. Carol Burnett, actress and comedian; Carol Channing, actress and singer; Carole King, singer and songwriter. **Carey, Cari, Carleen, Carlene, Carley, Caro, Carole, Carroll, Karol, Karyl, Lola, Lolita, Lottie, Sharleen, Sharlene, Sherry, Sheryl**

Caroline (Italian) "Strong and womanly." Feminine form of Charles. Caroline Kennedy, daughter of John F. Kennedy; Princess Caroline of Monaco. **Carlyn, Carolin, Carolina, Carolyn, Carolynn, Carolynne, Karla, Karolina, Karoline, Karolyn**

Caron (Welsh) "Loved one." **Carron, Karen**

Carrie Form of Caroline. Main character in Theodore Dreiser's novel *Sister Carrie*. Carrie Fisher, actress. **Carey, Cari, Carie, Cary, Kari, Karrie**

Carson (Old English) "One who lives near a marsh." Carson McCullers, American writer. **Carsie, Carsy**

Casey (Irish Gaelic) "Vigilant one." **Caci, Case, Casie, Casy, Cayce, Kacie, Kacy**

Cassandra (Greek) "Helper of mankind." A form of Alexandra. In Greek mythology, Cassandra was the prophetic daughter of Priam and Hecuba. **Casandra, Cass, Cassandre, Cassey, Cassie, Kassandra, Kassey, Sandra, Sandy**

Cassidy (Irish Gaelic) "Clever" or "curly-haired one." **Cassie**

Catherine (Greek) "Pure one." English and French form of Katherine. Catherine Deneuve, actress. **Caitlin, Cat, Cate, Caterina, Catharine, Cathi, Cathie, Cathleen, Cathlene, Cathrine, Cathyrn, Cathy, Catrina, Catriona, Caty, Caye**

Cecilia (Latin) "One who is unable to see." Feminine form of

Cecil. St. Cecilia, patron saint of music. Name of famous song by Simon and Garfunkel. Cicely Tyson, actress. **Cece, Cecelia, Cecile, Ceil, Cele, Celia, Celina, Celine, Cicely, Cissy, Sisile, Sissy**

Celeste (Latin) "From heaven" or "heavenly." Celeste Holm, actress. **Cele, Celesta, Celestia, Celestina, Celestine, Celestyn, Celia, Celisse, Celka**

Chandra (Sanskrit) "Moonlike."

Chantal (French) "Of the stony place." (Latin) "Songlike." **Chandal, Chantalle, Chantel, Chantell, Shantal, Shantalle**

Charity (Latin) "Benevolent, charitable one." A Puritan virtue name. **Carissa, Charissa, Charita, Charry, Cherri, Cherry**

Charleen (English) Form of Charlotte. **Charlene, Charline, Sharleen, Sharlene**

Charlotte (French) "Small, womanly one." Feminine form of Charles. Charlotte Brontë, English writer. **Carla, Carlotta, Charla, Charlene, Charlotta, Cheril, Cherlyn, Cheryl, Karla, Karlotta, Lola, Lolita, Lottie, Sharlene, Sharline, Sherry, Sheryl**

Charmaine (Latin) "Little one's song." Form of Carmen. **Charmain, Sharmain**

Chastity (Latin) "Virginal one." Chastity Bono, daughter of Sonny and Cher.

Chaya (Hebrew) "Of life." Feminine form of Chaim. **Chava, Hava, Haya**

Chelsea (Old English) "From the ship's landing place." Chelsea Noble, actress. **Chelsey, Chelsie, Chesley**

Cherie (French) "Loved one." **Cher, Chere, Cherey, Cheri, Cherice, Cherise, Cherish, Cherry, Sherry**

Cheryl (American) Form of Carol or Charlotte. Cher and Cheryl Ladd, actresses; Cheryl Tiegs, model and actress. **Cher, Cherelle, Cherene**

Chiquita (Spanish) "Small one." **Chick, Chickie, Chicky**

Chloe (Greek) "Young green bloom." Name of the Greek goddess of agriculture. Cloris Leachman, actress and comedienne. **Chloris, Cloe, Cloris**

Christabel (Latin) "A beautiful Christian." **Belle, Christa, Christabelle, Christy, Ella**

Christine (Latin) "A Christian" or "an anointed one." Chris Evert, tennis player; Christie Brinkley, model; Christine Lahti, actress; Christina Onassis, heiress. **Chris, Chrissie, Christa, Christan, Christel, Christi, Christian, Christi-**

ana, Christie, Christin, Christina, Christy, Christye, Cris, Crystal, Kirsten, Kris, Kristen, Kristi, Tina

Cinderella (French) "Small one from the ashes." The name is from the famous fairy tale. **Cindi, Cindy, Ella**

Clara (Latin) "Bright, illustrious one." Clara Barton, founder of the American Red Cross; Clare Booth Luce, magazine publisher and writer. **Clair, Claire, Clare, Clarette, Clarey, Clari, Clarice, Clarinda, Clary**

Clarice (French) "Clear, bright one." Clarice Taylor, actress. **Cherissa, Clarise, Clarissa**

Claudia (Latin) "Lame one." Feminine form of Claude. Claudette Colbert, actress. **Claudelle, Claudette, Claudie, Claudina, Claudine, Gladys**

Clementine (Greek) "Merciful." Best known by the song of the same name. **Clem, Clemence, Clementia, Clementina, Clemmie, Clemmy**

Cleo (Greek) "Famed or glorious one." Short form of Cleopatra, name of the famous Egyptian queen. **Clea, Cleopatra, Clio**

Cody (Old English) "A cushion." **Codee, Codie**

Colette (French) "Young, victorious one." Short form of Nicoletta. Well known because of the French writer Colette (Sidonie-Gabrielle Colette). **Coletta, Collette**

Colleen (Irish Gaelic) "Girlish." Colleen Dewhurst, actress; Colleen McCullough, novelist. **Coleen, Colene, Collie, Colline**

Concetta (Italian) Perhaps referring to "one like the Virgin Mary who conceives immaculately." **Concepción, Concha, Conchata, Concheta, Conchita**

Constance (Latin) "Faithful and firm." Connie Stevens, singer. **Connie, Conny, Constancia, Constantia, Constantine, Costanza**

Consuela (Spanish) "One who comforts or consoles," referring to the title of the Virgin Mary, "Our Lady of Solace." **Consolata, Consuelo**

Cora (Greek) "A maiden." Coretta Scott King, civil rights activist and wife of Martin Luther King, Jr. **Corabel, Corella, Corena, Corene, Coretta, Corette, Corey, Corina, Corine, Corinne, Corissa**

Coral (Latin) "Coral." **Coralee, Coralie, Coraline**

Cordelia (Welsh) "A jewel from the sea." (Latin) "Gentle-hearted." The youngest daughter in Shakespeare's *King Lear*. **Cordie, Cordula, Cordy, Corula, Delia**

Corliss (Old English) "Cheerful, good-natured one." **Colise, Corlie, Corly**

Cornelia (Latin) "Hornlike." Feminine form of Cornelius. **Cornela, Cornelle, Cornie, Corny, Nelia, Nell, Nellie, Nelly, Nina**

Cosette (French) "From the victorious people." **Cosetta**

Cosima (Greek) "Harmonious one" or "of the ordered universe." **Cosme, Kosma**

Courtney (Old English) "Of the court." An aristocratic British surname popular today as a given female name. **Cortney, Courtenay, Courtnay**

Crystal (Latin) "Clear as ice." Crystal Gayle, singer. **Christal, Chrystal, Cristal, Krystal**

Cybil (Greek) "A knowing woman or prophetess." Cybil Shepherd, actress. **Cybele, Cybill, Sibyl**

Cynthia (Greek) "Of the moon." Another name for the Greek goddess Artemis, who was born on Mount Cynthos. Cindy Crawford, model; Cyndi Lauper, singer. **Cindy, Cyndi, Cynth, Cynthie, Cynthy, Sindee**

Cyrena (Greek) "One from Cyrene." In Greek mythology, Cyrene is a water nymph much favored by Apollo. **Cyrene**

Cyrilla (Latin) "Lordly one." Feminine form of Cyrus. **Ciri, Cirilla**

GIRLS
D

Dacia (Greek) "One from Dacia." (Irish Gaelic) "From the South." **Dacey, Dacie, Dacy, Dasey, Dasie, Dasy**

Dagmar (Scandinavian) "A day maid." (Old German) "A glory of the Danes." A name of Danish royalty. **Dagare, Mar**

Dahlia (Scandinavian) "From the dale or valley." A flower so named to honor the Swedish botanist Anders Dahl. **Dalia**

Daisy (Old English) "Born on the day's eye." **Daisey, Daisie, Dasey, Dasi, Dasie**

Dale (Old English) "Of the dale or valley." **Dael, Daile, Dayle**

Dallas (Irish Gaelic) "Wise and gentle one." (Old English) "From the estate in the valley." **Dallis**

Damaris (Greek) "Calflike." **Damara, Damaress, Dameris, Damiris, Mara, Tamaris**

Damita (Spanish) "Small, noble woman." **Damite, Damitie**

Dana (Scandinavian) "From Denmark." **Dayna**

Danielle (Hebrew) "One whose judge is God." Feminine form of Daniel. **Daniele, Daniella, Danni, Dannie, Danny, Danya, Danyelle**

Danika (Slavic) "The morning star." **Danica**

Daphne (Greek) "Laurel or bay leaf." In Greek mythology, the name was held by a nymph whose father changed her into a laurel tree to escape the attentions of Apollo. Daphne Du Maurier, English novelist. **Daffi, Daffie, Daffy, Daphney, Daphny**

Dara (Hebrew) "Compassionate one." **Darah, Darya**

Darcy (Irish Gaelic) "Dark one." **Darcey, Darci**

Darlene (Old French) "Dear little one." Darryl Hannah, actress. **Darelle, Darleen, Darline, Darryl**

Daria (Persian) "Prosperous one." Feminine form of Darius. **Dari, Darice, Darie, Darina, Darya, Dasha**

Davine (Hebrew) "Well-loved one." Feminine form of David. **Daveta, Davida, Davidine, Davina, Davita, Veda, Vida, Vita, Vitia**

Davon (Irish Gaelic) "Great one." Feminine form of Darren.

Dawn (Old English) "Beginning of the day." **Daun**

Deanna (Latin) "Schoolmistress." (Old English) "From the valley." Feminine form of Dean. Deanna Durbin, actress. **Deana, Deanne, Dena, Denna, Dina**

Deborah (Hebrew) Biblical name meaning "beelike," referring to the industriousness of bees and the perfection of female bees. Debbie Boone, singer; Debbie Reynolds, actress and singer; Deborah Harry, singer; Debra Winger, actress. **Deb, Debbie, Debbo, Debby, Debi, Debor, Debora, Debra, Devorah**

Decima (Latin) "Tenth child." Common Roman name given to the tenth child born. Decima was the Roman goddess of childbirth.

Deirdra (Irish Gaelic) "One of sorrow." Legendary Irish heroine who was betrothed to a king but instead eloped with her lover. In retaliation, the king murdered her lover, and Deidra died of a broken heart. **Dede, Dedra, Dee, Deedee, Deirde, Didi**

Delia (Greek) "From the Isle of Delos." The birthplace of the goddess Artemis. **Dee, Dehlia, Delinda, Didi**

Delicia (Latin) "Delightful one." **Delice, Delise**

Delilah (Hebrew) Biblical name meaning "beautiful, amorous one who appeals for sympathy." Delilah was Samson's mistress and ultimately his betrayer. **Dalilia, Delila, Lila, Lilah**

Delphine (Greek) "From Delphi," which for Greeks was considered to be the "womb of the earth." The name can also be used to signify the flower delphinium. **Delfina, Delfine, Delphina**

Demetria (Greek) "Of the fertile land," referring to Demeter, Greek goddess of the harvest. Demi Moore, actress. **Demeter, Demetra, Demetris, Demi**

Denise (Greek) "One who follows Dionysus," the Greek god of wine. Feminine form of Dennis. Denise Levertov, U.S. poet. **Denice, Dennie, Denny, Denyce, Denyse**

Desdemona (Greek) "Ill-fated one." Desdemona is the tragic

Four million babies were born in the United States last year, the largest number in a single birth year since the early sixties. Some parents seem to worry that original names are in short supply.

Take the case of Tanyce Alaga-Bowen, recently reported in *The Wall Street Journal*. Her son was named Nicholas at first. Then she changed it to Darius and a few weeks later to Orion ("but he really didn't have the look of an Orion"). So today, Tanyce Alaga-Bowen's son's name is Danaan Alaga-Bowen.

There are other offbeat names you might try. There's always the old tried and true Zappa family favorites: Moon Unit and Dweezil. Or Joan Didion's eldest daughter's rather exceptional name, Quintana Roo. The longest personal name on record, according to the *Guinness Book of World Records,* is Rhoshandiatel-lyneshiaunneveshenk. You may choose to name your son Cuchulain, after a mythical Irish warrior.

But first you might place a call to Albert Mehrabian, a psychology professor at UCLA, who counsels patients who are unhappy with their names. He has discovered that some parents don't realize the impact unusual names can have on their children. Among his many patients are a girl named Fayle (pronounced Fail) and boys named Lovie and Magnum.

So beware of the connotations when you bestow an offbeat name.

---

heroine of Shakespeare's *Othello*. **Desdamona, Desmona, Mona** Desirée (French) "One desired or wished for." **Desire**

Deva (Sanskrit) "Divine." **Devi**

Devan (Irish Gaelic) "One who writes poetry." **Devina, Devinna, Devinne, Devon, Devona**

Dever (Old French) "Crystal-like." **DeVer, Deverre**

Devona (Old English) "From Devonshire." **Devondra, Devonna**

Diana (Latin) "Divine one." Diana is the Roman goddess of the hunt, the moon, and fertility. Diane Arbus, photographer; Diahann Carroll, Diane Keaton, and Dianne Wiest, actresses; Diana Ross, singer; Diana Spencer Windsor, princess of Wales. **Deana, Deanna, Dede, Dee, Dena, Di, Diahann, Dian, Diandra, Diane, Dianna, Dianne, Didi, Dion, Dyana, Dyane, Dyann, Dyanna, Dyanne**

Dinah (Hebrew) Bible name meaning "one who is vindicated." The daughter of Leah and Jacob whose rape by Shechem was avenged by her brothers. Dinah Shore, singer and actress; Dina Merrill, actress. **Dena, Dina, Dynah**

Dionne (Greek) "Gift of God." In Greek mythology, Dione is the mother of Aphrodite. Dionne Warwicke, popular singer; Dyan Cannon, actress. **Dione, Dionis, Dyan, Dyonne**

Disa (Scandinavian) "A goddess." **Lisa**

Dixie (French) "Tenth child." (American) "Girl born in the South." Term for the American South. **Dix**

Dolores (Spanish) "Sorrowful one," referring to a title for the Virgin Mary, Maria de los Doloras, (Mary of Sorrows). Dolly Parton, singer and actress. **Delora, Delores, Deloris, Delorita, Dolly, Lola, Lolita**

Dominique (Latin) "One who belongs to God." Feminine form of Dominic. **Dominga, Domini, Dominica**

Donna (Latin) "Lady of the house." (Italian) "My respectful lady." Donna Karen, fashion designer; Donna Reed, actress; Donna Summer, singer. **Donella, Donelle, Donia, Donis, Donnie, Donny**

Dorcas (Greek) Biblical name meaning "gazellelike," referring to their graceful swiftness and their soft, lustrous eyes. **Dorchas**

Doreen (Irish Gaelic) "Sullen." **Dorene, Dorine**

Doris (Greek) "A gift." (Latin) "A freed woman." In Greek mythology, Doris is a minor goddess of the sea. Doris Day, actress; Doris Lessing, British writer. **Dora, Doralin, Dorelia, Dori, Doria, Dorice, Dorisa, Dorise, Dorita, Dorri, Dorrie, Dorris, Dorry, Dory**

Dorothy (Greek) "God's gift." Dorothy Hamill, Olympic ice skater; Dorothy is the heroine in *The Wizard of Oz*. **Dode, Dody, Dollie, Dolly, Dora, Dori, Dorothea, Dorrit, Dorthea, Dorthy, Dory, Dot, Dottie, Dotty**

Drew (English) "Womanly one." Short feminine form

of Andrew. Drew Barrymore, actress. **Dru, Druey, Druie**

Drina (Spanish) "Helper of mankind." Form of Alexandra. **Drisa, Drise**

Drusilla (Latin) Biblical name meaning "of great beauty." **Drucella, Drucilla, Druscella, Drewsila**

Dulcie (Latin) "Sweet one." **Dulce, Dulcine, Dulsie**

GIRLS
E

Earlene (Old English) "A noble woman." Feminine form of Earl. **Earla, Earleen, Earley, Erlene, Erline**

Eartha (Old English) "Born of the earth." Eartha Kitt, singer and actress. **Erda, Ertha, Herta, Hertha**

Easter (Old English) "Child born on Easter."

Ebony (Egyptian) "Of the deep, black woods." **Ebbony, Ebonee, Eboney, Eboni, Ebonie**

Eden (Hebrew) Biblical place name meaning "pleasant and delightful." Oftentimes biblical place names were used for naming women because there are so few female names in the Bible. **Eddie, Edin**

Edith (Old English) "Generous and elaborate gift." Edith Piaf, French singer; Edith Wharton, English novelist. **Dita, Eda, Ede, Edi, Edie, Edita, Editha, Edithe, Ediva, Edy, Edyth, Edythe, Eydie**

Edna (Hebrew) "Rejuvenated and pleasurable." **Eddi, Eddie, Eddy**

Edrea (Old English) "Prosperous; powerful." **Edrena**

Edwina (Old English) "Prosperous friend." Feminine form of Edwin. Edwina Mountbatten, countess of Burma. **Edina, Edwardine, Edweena, Edwyna**

Eileen (Irish) "Bright, shining one." Form of Helen. **Aileen, Eilean, Eiley, Ilene**

Elaine (Old French) "Bright one." (Welsh) "Fawnlike." Form of Helen. **Elaina, Elana, Elane, Elayne, Laine, Lainey, Lane**

Eldora (Spanish) "Golden or gilded one." **Eldoria**

Eleanor (Greek) "Shining one." (Old German) "Bright, foreign one." Form of Helen. Eleanor Roosevelt, lecturer, writer, and wife of thirty-second U.S. president. **Eleanora, Eleanore, Elenore, Elinor, Elinore, Ella, Elle, Ellen, Ellie, Elora, Leanora, Lena, Lenore, Leonora, Nell, Nellie, Nelly, Nora**

Electra (Greek) "Brilliant, bright one." In Greek mythology, Electra is the daughter of Agamemnon, who, with her brother Orestes, avenges her father's death. **Elettra**

Eliora (Hebrew) "My light is the lord." **Eleora, Elyse, Elysia**

Elise (French) Form of Elizabeth. **Elissa, Elyssa, Lissa, Lissie**

Elita (Latin-French) "Chosen one." **Elata**

Elizabeth (Hebrew) Biblical name meaning "one who believes in God as perfection." The mother of John the Baptist. Elizabeth I and II, queens of England; Elizabeth Taylor and Elizabeth Montgomery, actresses. **Bell, Bess, Bessie, Bessy, Beth, Betsy, Bette, Bettina, Bettine, Betty, Elisa, Elisabet, Elisabeth, Elise, Elissa, Eliza, Elsa, Elsbeth, Else, Elspet, Elyse, Isabel, Lib, Libbey, Libby, Lisa, Lisabeth, Lise, Lisette, Lissa, Lissy, Liz, Liza, Lizabeth, Lizbeth, Lizzie, Lizzy, Lusa**

Ella (Old German) "All others," referring to foreigners. (Old English) "A fairy maiden." Ella Fitzgerald, singer. **Ellette, Ellie, Elly**

Ellen (English) Form of Helen. Ellen Burstyn, actress. **Ellie, Elly, Ellyn**

Elmira (Old English) "Of famous nobility."

Eloise (French) Form of Heloise or Louise. Because of the famous love letters written between Eloise and Abelard in the twelfth century, the name has come to refer to "one who is pious and faithful." **Eloisa, Heloise**

Elsa (Old German) "Noble one." **Else, Elsie, Elsy, Ilsa, Ilse**

Elvira (Old German) "An elf counselor." (Latin) "White one." **Elva, Elvera, Elvina, Elvire, Elwira**

Emily (Latin) "Eager, competitive one." Emily Dickinson, American poet. **Amalea, Amalia, Amalie, Amelia, Em, Emalee, Emalia, Emelda, Emelia, Emilee, Emilie, Emiline, Emmi, Emmie, Emmy, Emyle**

Emma (Old German) "All-embracing one." Emma Willard,

educator. **Em, Ema, Emmaline, Emmalynn, Emma-lynne, Emmeline, Emmy**

Enid (Welsh) "Purity of soul." Enid Nemy, writer and journalist. **En, Enit**

Erica (Scandinavian) "Ever-powerful one." Feminine form of Eric. Erica Jong, writer. **Enrica, Enrika, Enricha, Ericka, Ricca, Ricki, Rickie, Ricky, Rikki**

Erin (Irish Gaelic) "From Ireland." Used as a poetic name for Ireland. **Aaren, Aryn, Eran, Erina, Erinn, Erinna, Eryn**

Erma (Old German) "Whole one." Erma Bombeck, writer. **Ermina, Erminia, Irma**

Ernestine (Old English) "Earnest one." Ernestine Schumann-Heink, opera singer. **Erna, Ernesta**

Esme (Latin) "Esteem." **Esma, Esmee, Esmie**

Esmeralda (Spanish) "Emeraldlike." (Latin) "One who is well esteemed." Darrin Stevens's mother-in-law on the TV show *Bewitched*. **Emerald, Esma, Esme, Ezmeralda**

Estelle (Old French) "Starlike." **Estele, Estell, Estella, Estrella, Stella**

Esther (Hebrew) Biblical name meaning "star." (Persian) "Myrtle." Name of a historical Jewish maiden who became the wife of a Persian king. Through her gift of persuasion, she was able to save many Jews. Her Hebrew name, Hadassah, means "myrtle." Esther Williams, swimmer. **Essie, Esta, Ester, Hester, Hetta, Hettie, Hetty**

Ethel (Old German) "Of noble birth." Ethel Merman, actress. **Ethelda, Ethelin, Ethelinda, Ethyl, Ethyle**

Etta (Old German) "Small one." **Etty**

Eudora (Greek) "An honored gift." Eudora Welty, writer. **Dora, Dorrie, Dorry, Eudoria**

Eugenia (Greek) "Well born." A feminine form of Eugene. Eugenia Price, southern American writer. **Eugenie, Genia, Genie**

Eunice (Greek) "Victorious one." Eunice Kennedy Shriver. **Unice**

Euphemia (Greek) "One who is spoken well of." **Effie, Effy, Euphenie, Fanny, Phemie**

Eustacia (Greek) "Fruitful one." **Stacey, Stacia, Stacie, Stacy**

Eva (English) Form of Evangeline. Eva Gabor, actress. **Evita, Evonne**

Evangeline (Greek) "One who bears good news." **Eva, Evangelia, Evangelina, Eve, Vangie, Vangy**

Eve (Hebrew) Biblical name meaning "one who lives." In Western religions, the name of the first woman. **Eba, Eva, Evie, Evonne, Evy**

Evelyn (Irish Gaelic) "Bright one." **Aveline, Evelina, Eveline, Evelyne**

GIRLS
F

Faith (Latin) "One who is true and faithful." A Puritan virtue name. **Fae, Fay, Faye, Fayth, Faythe**

Fallon (Irish Gaelic) "Descended from the ruler."

Fanny (English) Form of Frances. Fanny Brice, entertainer; Fanny Farmer, entrepreneur. **Fan, Fannie**

Farrah (English) "Beautiful and happy one." Farrah Fawcett, actress. **Fara, Farah, Farra, Farrand, Fayre**

Fatima (Arabic) "One who abstains or weans." Fatimah was the Prophet Muhammad's favorite daughter. **Fatimah, Fatma**

Fawn (Old French) "Like a young deer." Fawn Hall, Oliver North's secretary.

Fay (Old French) "A fairy." Faye Dunaway, actress. **Fae, Faina, Faye, Fayette, Fayina**

Felicia (Latin) "Lucky one." Feminine form of Felix. **Felice, Felicity, Felis, Felise, Felisha, Phelicia, Philicia**

Fern (Old English) "Fernlike." Plant name used as a first name. Fern Arable is a character in E. B. White's *Charlotte's Web*. **Ferne**

Fernanda (Old German) "Adventuresome, daring." Feminine form of Ferdinand. **Ferdinanda, Ferdinande, Fernande, Fernandina**

Fidella (Latin) "One who is faithful." **Fidela, Fidele, Fidelity**

Fifi (French) "One whom God will give more children." Form of Josephine. **Fifina, Fifine**

Finella (Scottish Gaelic) "White-shouldered one." **Fenella, Fionnuala, Nuala**

Finlay (Irish Gaelic) "Fair-haired heroine." **Findlay, Findley, Finley**

Fiona (Irish Gaelic) "Fair-haired one." **Fenella, Finella, Fionna**

Fiorella (Italian) "Flowerlike."

Flannery (Old French) "A flat piece of metal." Flannery O'Connor, writer.

Flavia (Latin) "Blond-haired one." Roman clan name. **Flavian, Flavie, Flavien**

Fleur (French) "Flowerlike." **Fleurette**

Flora (Latin) "A flower." Flora Robson, English actress. **Fiora, Flo, Flor, Flore, Floria, Florrie, Florry**

Florence (Latin) "Flourishing, prosperous one." Florence Nightingale, founder of nursing. **Fiorenza, Flo, Florance, Florencia, Florinda, Florine, Floris, Flossie**

Florida (Latin) "Flowery, blooming."

Frances (Latin) "One with freedom" or "one from France." Feminine form of Francis. **Fanny, Ferike, Fran, Francesca, Francetta, Franci, Francie, Francine, Francoise, Francy, Franke, Frannie, Franny**

Francesca (Italian) Form of Frances. **Francisca, Frascuela**

Fredrica (Old German) "One who rules peacefully." Feminine form of Frederick. **Frederika, Fredi, Fredrika, Friederike, Fritzi, Fryda**

Freya (Scandinavian) "Honorable, noble woman." Scandinavian goddess of love and beauty. **Freja**

Frieda (Old German) "Of peaceful nobility." Frieda Lawrence, wife of D. H. Lawrence. **Elfrieda, Freda, Freeda, Frida, Winifred**

Fulvia (Latin) "Tawny-colored."

GIRLS
G

Gabrielle (Hebrew) "Worshiper of God." Feminine form of Gabriel. Gabriela Sabatini, tennis player. **Gabie, Gaby, Gabriela, Gabriella, Gabrila, Gavra, Gavrielle**

Gail (Old English) "A source of joy." Form of Abigail. **Gael, Gale, Gayle**

Galina (Russian) "Of the light." **Gala, Galinka, Galya, Gayle, Gayleen, Gaylene**

Garland (Old French) "A wreath or garland of flowers."

Garnette (Middle English) "The garnet gemstone." **Garnet, Garnetta**

Gavrila (Hebrew) "A heroine." **Gavriella, Gavrielle**

Gay (Old French) "Merry, lively one." **Gae, Gai, Gala, Galina, Gaye**

Gaynor (Welsh) Form of Guinevere. **Gayna, Gaynah, Gayner**

Gemma (Italian) "Gemlike one." **Gema, Gemmie, Jemma**

Gene (English) Short form of Eugenia. **Genia**

Genevieve (Celtic-French) "From the group of pure, white women." St. Genevieve is the patron saint of Paris. **Gena, Geneva, Gennie, Genny, Gina, Jennie, Jenny**

Georgia (Latin) "One who works the land." Feminine form of George. Georgia O'Keefe, artist. **George, Georgeanna, Georgeanne, Georgena, Georgene, Georgette, Georgia, Georgiana, Georgina, Georgine, Giorgia**

Geraldine (Old German) "Mighty warrior woman." Feminine form of Gerald. Geraldine Ferraro, politician; Geraldine Page, actress. **Dina, Geraldina, Gerri, Gerrie, Gerry, Giralda, Jeri, Jerri, Jerry**

Gerda (Scandinavian) "From the protected estate." In Old Norse mythology, the beautiful Gerd and her husband, Frey, are fertility gods. **Garsha, Gerd, Gerde, Gerdi**

■ LET THE LAST BE FIRST! ■

Time was when people had first names and last names.

There were always strange enclaves, usually among the polo-playing set, where anomalies arose, such as strong young lads with first names like . . . well, Pierce, or Lathrop or Mortimer, and debutantes named Buffy (for Brennan) or Muffy (for McAllister) or Binky (for who knows what?).

But for the most part, everybody could tell your first name from your last name. Joe and Jack, Sue or Nancy, these were first names; Bradley or Harrison, Avery or Courtney, these were last names.

There were a few handy exceptions—notably, a middle name was fair game. If your wife felt a special closeness to her grandfather, George Remington, your daughter could be given the middle name of Remington without blurring the lines or creating an identity crisis.

No more! The latest craze is for letting the last be first. Addisons, Blakes, Parkers, and Walkers of both sexes abound, from the polo field to the subdivision.

What follows is a list of increasingly popular first names that have evolved from last names:

GIRLS	BOYS
Ainsley	Abbott
Arden	Anderson
Avery	Barclay
Brook	Bartlett
Courtney	Bennett
Greer	Caldwell
Hadley	Chadwick
Hailey	Claybourne
Jordan	Donovan
Laine	Frasier
Mackenzie	Griffith
Mallory	Huntington
Morgan	Lyman
Paige	Merrick
Shelby	Montgomery
Sheridan	Parker

Sloan	Sanford
Tatum	Sterling
Taylor	Thayer
Whitney	Woodrow

Germaine (Latin) "A German" or "a brother," referring probably to the idea of Christian brotherhood. Feminine form of Germain. **Germain, Germana, Jermaine**

Gertrude (Old German) "Mighty woman ruler." Gertrude Stein, English writer and intellect; Gertrude Vanderbilt Whitney, sculptor. **Geert, Gert, Gertie, Gertraud, Gertrud, Gertruda, Gertrudis, Gerty, Gig, Trude, Trudi, Trudy**

Gianna (Italian) "Gracious one." Feminine form of Giovanni (John). **Gianetta, Gianina, Giannina**

Gigi (French) Form of Georgina.

Gila (Hebrew) "One whose joy is eternal." The daughter of Rigoletto in Verdi's opera *Rigoletto*. **Gilada, Gilah, Gilia**

Gilberta (Old German) "From a famous pledge." Feminine form of Gilbert. **Gilberte, Gilbertina, Gilbertine, Gillie, Gilly**

Gilda (Old German) "Sacrificial." (Old English) "Covered with gold." Gilda Radner, actress and comedienne.

Gillian (Latin) "Youthful one." **Gill, Gillia, Gillie, Gilly, Jill, Julia, Juliana**

Gina (English) Form of Eugenia or Regina. Gina Lollobrigida and Geena Davis, actresses. **Geena, Jena**

Ginger (English) "One with ginger-colored hair." Used also as a nickname for someone with a hot or "gingery" temper. Ginger Rogers, entertainer.

Ginny (English) Short form of Virginia. **Ginia, Ginnie**

Giselle (Old German) "One who is pledged or promised to another." **Gisa, Gisela, Gisele, Gisella, Gizela**

Gladys (Welsh) "Lame or frail one." Form of Claudia. Gladys Knight, rhythm and blues singer. **Glad, Gladi, Gleda**

Glenda (Old Welsh) "Pure and good." Glenn Close and Glenda Jackson, actresses. **Glenn, Glenna, Glennis, Glynis, Glynnie, Glynnis**

Gloria (Latin) "Glorious one." Gloria Swanson, actress; Gloria Steinem, political activist. **Glori, Gloriana, Gloriane, Glory**

Godiva (Old English) "Gift of God." The legendary Lady Godiva, an eleventh-century Mercian noblewoman who rode naked on horseback through town in hopes of persuading her husband not to impose a tax on the townspeople.

Golda (Old English) "Golden one." Golda Meir, Israeli prime minister; Goldie Hawn, actress. **Gilda, Goldie, Goldy**

Grace (Latin) "Attractive and graceful." Princess Grace of Monaco (Grace Kelly Grimaldi). **Gracey, Gracia, Gracie, Gratia, Gratiana, Grayce, Grazia**

Greer (English) Form of Gregoria. Greer Garson, actress. **Grier**

Gregoria (Latin) "Vigilant one." Feminine form of Gregory.

Gretchen (German) "Pearl-like." Form of Margaret. Greta Garbo, actress. **Greta, Grete, Gretel**

Griselda (Old German) "A gray-haired woman warrior." **Griseldis, Grishilda, Grizelda, Selda, Zelda**

Gudrun (Scandinavian) "One with the secret knowledge of God." **Gudren, Gudrin, Guro**

Guida (Italian) "A guide or teacher." (Old German) "Warrior maiden."

Guinevere (Welsh) "Blessed fair-haired one." The legendary wife of King Arthur. **Genevieve, Genna, Genni, Gennie, Genny, Guenevere, Guenna, Guinna, Jen, Jenifer, Jenni, Jennie, Jennifer, Jenny, Winnie, Winny**

Gweldolyn (Welsh) "Beautiful white-browed one." **Gwen, Gwenda, Gwendaline, Gwendolen, Gwendoline, Gwenith, Gwenneth, Gwennie, Gwyn, Gwyneth, Gwynne, Wendie, Wendy, Wynette, Wynne**

Gypsy (Old English) "One who wanders aimlessly." Gypsy Rose Lee, singer. **Gipsy**

GIRLS
H

Hadassah (Hebrew) "Myrtlelike." The Hebrew name of the biblical queen Esther. **Dassah**

Hagar (Hebrew) Biblical name meaning "one who takes flight or leaves." Hagar was the trusted handmaiden to Sarah, Abraham's wife. Since Sarah was barren, she let Hagar conceive a child by Abraham. Once done, Sarah, resenting Hagar, abused her, and Hagar took flight. **Haggar**

Haidee (Greek) "Modest one." Character in Byron's poem *Don Juan*. **Heidi**

Hallie (Greek) "Thinking of the sea." **Halli, Hally**

Hannah (Hebrew) Biblical name meaning "graceful, favored one," referring, perhaps, to God favoring one with a child. Hannah is the mother of the prophet Samuel. Hana Mandlikova, tennis player. **Ann, Anna, Hana, Hanna, Hanny, Nan, Nanny**

Hansine (German) "Gracious one." Feminine form of Hans. **Hansi, Hansie**

Happy (English) "A happy, merry child."

Harley (Old English) "From the longfield." **Harlene, Harli, Harlie**

Harmony (Latin) "Harmonious one." **Harmonia, Harmonie**

Harper (English) "One who plays a harp." Harper Lee, author of *To Kill a Mockingbird*.

Harriet (French) "One who rules the home." Feminine form of Harry. Harriet Beecher Stowe, author. **Harrietta, Harriette, Harriot, Harriott, Hattie, Hatty**

Haven (Dutch) "Harbor." **Hagen**

Haya (Hebrew) "Life." Feminine form of Hyam.

Hayley (Old English) "From the meadow full of hay." Hayley Mills, actress. **Hailey, Haley, Halie**

Hazel (Old English) "One with the coloring of hazelnuts." **Aveline**

Heather (Middle English) "From the heaths." Heather Locklear, actress. **Heath**

Hebe (Greek) "Youthful one." Name of the Greek goddess of youth.

Hedda (Old German) "One who tends to quarrel and debate." Hedda is the heroine of Henrik Ibsen's play *Hedda Gabler*. **Edda, Heda, Heddie, Hede, Hedi, Hedvig, Hedvika, Hedwig, Hedy**

Heidi (German) "Of noble birth." Popular form of Adelaide. Heidi is the main character in the popular children's story of the same title by Johanna Spyri. **Heida, Heide**

Helen (Greek) "One who illuminates the spirit." In Greek mythology, the Trojan War was fought over the beautiful Helene, wife of Menelaus. St. Helena, the mother of Constantine the Great, is attributed with discovering the True Cross. Helen Hayes, actress; Helen Keller, blind and deaf educator and author; Helen Reddy, singer. **Aileen, Elaine, Elane, Eleanore, Elenore, Ella, Ellen, Ellie, Ellyn, Helena, Helene, Helyn, Ielena, Lana, Lena, Lenka, Lenore, Leonora, Leonore, Leora, Lora, Nell, Nellie, Nelly, Nora, Norah**

Helga (Scandinavian) "Pious, religious one." **Olga**

Helma (Old German) "Helmeted, protected one." **Helmine, Hilma, Mina**

Heloise (French) Form of Eloise.

Henrietta (French) "Ruler of the home." Feminine form of Henry. **Etta, Etti, Ettie, Etty, Hattie, Hatty, Hendrika, Henrieta, Henriette, Henryette, Hetti, Hettie, Hetty, Yetta**

Hephzibah (Hebrew) Biblical name meaning "my delight is this child." Hephzibah was the wife of Hezekiah, the king of Judah. **Hephsibah, Hepsey, Hepsie, Hepzibah**

Hera (Greek) "Queenly one." In Greek mythology, Hera is the wife of Zeus and queen of the heavens.

Hermione (Greek) "Child of the earth." Feminine form of Herman or Hermes, the Greek messenger god. Hermione is the daughter of Helene of Troy. **Erma, Hermia, Hermina, Hermine, Herminia**

Hermosa (Spanish) "Beautiful one."

Hester (Spanish) "Starlike." Form of Esther. Hester Prynne, heroine of Nathaniel Hawthorne's *The Scarlett Letter*. **Hestia, Hettia**

Hilary (Latin) "Cheerful one." **Hillary, Hilliary**

Hilda (Old German) "Battle maiden." Name of an eleventh-century saint, St. Hildegard. **Hildagard, Hildagarde, Hilde, Hildegard, Hildegarde, Hildy**

Hinde (Hebrew) "Like a young deer." Feminine form of Hirsh. **Hinda, Hynda**

Holly (Old English) "Holly tree" or "holy one." A name given to girls born around Christmas. Holly Hunter, actress. **Holli, Hollie**

Honey (Old English) "Sweet one." **Honi**

Honor (Latin) "Woman of honor." Honor Blackman, actress. **Honner, Honnor, Honora, Honoria, Honour**

Hope (Old English) "One who has hope," referring probably to the hope of eternal life after death. A Puritan virtue name.

Horatia (Latin) "One who keeps time." Feminine form of Horace. **Horacia**

Hortense (Latin) "One who works in the garden." Hortense Calisher, writer. **Hortensia, Ortensia**

Huette (Old English) "Intelligent, spirited one." Feminine form of Hugh. **Huetta, Hugetta**

Hyacinth (Greek) "Beautiful young one." In Greek mythology, Hyacinth was a young boy much beloved by Apollo but whom Apollo accidentally killed. From his blood came a flower bearing his name. **Cinthie, Cynthia, Cynthie, Hyacintha, Hyacinthe, Hyacinthia, Jacinda, Jacintha, Jacinthe, Jacinta, Jackie, Jacky**

GIRLS
I

Iantha (Greek) "A flower of purple color." **Ianthina**

Ida (Old English) Prosperous one." (Old German) "Hardworking one." **Idalia, Idalina, Idaline, Idel, Idelle, Idette**

Iesha (Arabic) "Womanly." **Aisha, Ieashina, Ieesha, Ieeshia**

Ignatia (Latin) "Ardent, fiery one." Feminine form of Ignatius.

Ilana (Modern Hebrew) "Treelike."

Ilene (English) "Bright, shining one." Form of Eileen. **Ileane, Iline**

Ilona (Hungarian) "Beautiful, bright one." Form of Helen. **Ilka**

Ilse (German) Form of Elizabeth.

Imelda (Old German) "An all-encompassing battle maiden." Imelda Marcos, wife of the ex-dictator of the Philippines. **Imalda**

Imogen (Latin) "Lastborn," "innocent one," or "an image or likeness to." Imogen Cunningham, photographer. **Emogene, Imogene, Imogine**

Ina (Latin) "One who is motherlike." Originally used as a suffix for Italian and Spanish names to transform them from masculine to feminine.

India (English) The country name as a first name. India Wilkes, character in Margaret Mitchell's *Gone With the Wind;* India Hicks, granddaughter of Lord Mountbatten; Indira Gandhi, Indian political leader. **Indira**

Inez (Spanish) "Pure, virginal one." Form of Agnes. **Ines, Inesita, Innes, Ynes, Ynez**

Ingrid (Scandinavian) "Beautiful daughter of the fertile one." In Norse mythology, Ing is the god of the harvest, of prosperity, and of fertility. Ingrid Bergman, Swedish actress. **Inga, Ingaberg, Ingaborg, Inge, Inger**

Iolanthe (Greek) "A violet flower or jewel." **Iola, Iona, Ione, Ionia**

Irene (Greek) "Peaceful one." In Greek mythology, Irene is the goddess of peace. **Eirene, Erena, Irena, Irina, Rena, Renée, Rina**

Iris (Greek) "Like the flower" or "symbolic of the rainbow." Iris Murdoch, English writer. **Irisa, Irita**

Irma (Old German) "Powerful one." (Latin) "Noble." **Erma, Irmina**

Isabel (Spanish) Form of Elizabeth. Isabella Rossellini, actress and model. **Bell, Bella, Belle, Ibby, Isa, Isabell, Isabella, Isabelle, Isbel, Isobel, Izzie, Izzy, Sabella, Ysabel**

Isadora (Greek) "Gift of Isis." Isis is the Egyptian fertility goddess and mother of all things. Isadora Duncan, American dancer. **Dora, Dori, Dory, Isidora, Issy, Izzy**

Isis (Egyptian) "The ruling goddess."

Isolde (Welsh) "Fair one." Name of a young princess in the Arthurian legend whose romance with Tristam has tragic consequences. **Isold, Isolda, Isolte, Yseult, Ysolde**

Ita (Irish Gaelic) "Thirsty one." **Itala**

Ivana (Russian) Feminine form of Ivan or John. Ivana Trump, socialite. **Iva, Ivane**

Ivory (Latin) "Made of ivory."

Ivy (English) "Like the plant," referring, perhaps, to the way in which the ivy vine clings or grows along the side of a permanent structure. **Ivey, Ivie, Ivoreen, Ivory**

GIRLS
J

Jacinta (Spanish) "Like a purple hyacinth flower." (Greek) "Beautiful youth." **Giacinta, Jacinth, Jacintha, Jacinthe**

Jacqueline (Old French) "A supplanter." Feminine form of Jacques. Jacqueline Kennedy Onassis, wife of 35th U.S. president and book editor; Jaclyn Smith and Jacqueline Bisset, actresses. **Jacalyn, Jackelyn, Jackie, Jacki, Jacklyn, Jacky, Jaclin, Jaclyn, Jacobina, Jacquelin, Jacqueline, Jacquelynn, Jacquelyn**

Jade (Spanish) "Like the green gemstone." Jade Jagger, daughter of singer Mick Jagger. **Jada, Jayde**

Jamie (Hebrew) Modern U.S. feminine form of James. Jamie Lee Curtis, actress. **Jaime, Jaimee, Jamee, Jami, Jayme**

Jamila (Arabic) "Beautiful one." **Jamaala, Jamahla, Jamalla, Jamelle**

Jane (Hebrew) "Gracious one" or "gracious gift of God." Feminine form of John. Lady Jane Grey, queen of England for nine days in 1553; Jane Austen, English novelist; Jane Fonda, actress; Jane Pauley, broadcast journalist. **Jaine, Jan, Jana, Janaye, Janeen, Janel, Janell, Janene, Janet, Janetta, Janette, Janey, Janice, Janie, Janina, Janine, Janis, Janih, Janka, Janna, Jannel, Jannelle, Janot, Jayne, Jean, Jeanette, Jeanie, Jenni, Jennie, Jenny, Jess, Jessie, Jinny, Joan, Joana, Joanna, Joanne, Joni, Sheena, Shena**

Janet Form of Jane. Janet Leigh, actress; Janis Joplin, American rock singer. **Janetta, Janette, Janice, Janina, Janis, Janot**

Jasmine (Persian) "Like the fragrant jasmine flower." **Jasmin, Jessamine, Jessamyn, Yasmin**

Jean (Old French) "Gracious one." Form of Jane. Jean Dixon, psychic adviser; Jean Harlow, actress; Jeanette MacDonald, singer and actress. **Gene, Jannika, Jeana, Jeane, Jeanetta, Jeanette, Jeanne, Jeannie, Jenette, Jennine, Sine**

Jemima (Hebrew) Biblical name meaning "one as bright as a dove." The name of one of the daughters of Job renowned for her beauty. Also, the name of a Beatrix Potter character in *The Tale of Jemima Puddleduck*. **Jamima, Jemimah, Jemma, Jemmima, Jemmy, Yomina**

Jena (Arabic) "A small bird." **Jenna**

Jennifer (Welsh) "Fair, white one." Form of Guinevere. The actress Jennifer Jones made the name popular in the 1940s but its huge popularity in recent years is probably due to the heroine of Erich Segal's novel *Love Story*. Jennifer Capriati, tennis player. **Genna, Genni, Gennie, Gennifer, Genny, Jen, Jeni, Jenifer, Jenni, Jennie, Jenny**

Jerry (Old German) "Woman warrior." Form of Geraldine. Jerry Hall, model. **Jeraldine, Jeremia, Jeri, Jerilee, Jerrie, Jeryl**

Jessica (Hebrew) Biblical name meaning "born of the grace of God." In the Bible the name appeared as Iscah or Jesca. Presumably Shakespeare turned this into Jessica for the character of Shylock's daughter in *The Merchant of Venice*. Jessica Tandy and Jessica Lange, actresses. **Jess, Jessalin, Jessalyn, Jesse, Jesselyn, Jessie, Jessika, Jessy**

Jewel (Old French) "Like a precious gem" or "joyful." **Jewell, Jewelle**

Jezebel (Hebrew) Biblical name meaning "chaste one." Name of the Phoenician wife of King Ahab who was so wicked that the name has come to mean "shameless or imprudent one." **Jezabel, Jezabelle**

Jill, Jillian (Latin) "Youthful one." Form of Gillian. Popularized by the nursery rhyme "Jack and Jill." Jill Clayburgh and Jill St. John, actresses. **Gillian, Jillene, Jilli, Jillie, Jilly**

Joan (Hebrew) "Gracious one." Form of Jane. Joan of Arc, religious heroine; Joan Baez, folk singer; Joan Crawford, actress; Joan Didion, writer; Joan Rivers, comedienne. **Jo, Jodi, Jody, Joni, Jonie**

Joanne (Latin) Form of Joan. Joanne Woodward, actress.

Jo-Ann, Joann, Jo'anne, Jo-anne, Joeann, Johanna, Johannah, Johannes

Jobina (Hebrew) "Persecuted one." Feminine form of Job. **Jobi, Jobie, Joby, Jobye, Joybyna**

Jocelyn (Latin) "Playful one." (Old English) "One who is just." Feminine form of Justin. **Jocelin, Joceline, Jocelyne, Joci, Josselyn, Joyce, Joycelin, Justine, Lyn**

Jody (English) Form of Joan and Judith. Jodie Foster, actress. **Jodi, Jodie**

Joelle (Hebrew) "One who believes that God is the Lord." Feminine form of Joel. **Joella, Joellen, Joelly, Joelyn**

Jolene (Modern English) "God will give you more children." Form of Josephine. **Jolean, Joleen, Jolyen, Jolyn**

Jolie (French) "Pretty one." **Joli, Joly**

Jonina (Hebrew) "Dovelike one." **Jonati, Jonnina**

Jordan (Hebrew) "To descend or flow downward," refering to the waters of the Jordan River, where Christ was baptized. **Jordain, Jordana, Jordena, Jorey, Jori, Jorie, Jorrie, Jorry, Jourdan**

Josephine (Hebrew) "God will give you more children." Josephine was the pet name of Napoleon's wife, Empress Marie Josephe Rose. Josephine Baker, entertainer. **Fifi, Fina, Jo, Josee, Josefina, Josephene, Josephina, Josette, Josi, Josie, Josy**

Joy (Latin) "Joyous one." Joie Lee, actress. **Joi, Joie, Joya, Joyann, Joye**

Joyce (Latin) "Merry, joyful one." Joyce Carol Oates, American writer; Dr. Joyce Brothers, psychologist. **Jocelyn, Joice, Joy, Joycelyn, Joyous**

Juanita (Spanish) Form of Jane. Feminine form of Juan. **Juana, Nita, Wanita**

Judith (Hebrew) Biblical name meaning "of Jewish descent" or "praised one." Judy Collins, singer; Judy Chicago, artist; Judy Garland, actress. **Jodi, Jodie, Jody, Jude, Judi, Judy**

Julia (Latin) "One who is youthful." Feminine form of Julius. Julia Child, French cooking master; Julie Andrews, actress and singer; Juliet Capulet, heroine of Shakespeare's *Romeo and Juliet;* Julie Harris, Juliette Lewis, and Julia Roberts, actresses. **Giulia, Julee, Juliana, Juliane, Julianne, Julie, Juliet, Juliette, Julina, Juline, Julita**

June (English) "One born in June." Name of the month used

as a first name. June Allyson and June Lockhart, actresses.
Junette, Junia, Juniata, Junieta

Juno (Latin) "Of the heavens." The Roman goddess of marriage, wife of Jupiter (god of the heavens), and queen of the goddesses. **Junita**

Justine (Latin) "One who is just." Feminine form of Justin. **Guistina, Justa, Justina, Justinn**

GIRLS
K

Kai (Scandinavian) "Henlike." **Kay, Ky, Kye, Kyle, Kylie**

Kala (Hindu) "Black" or "time."

Kalila (Arabic) "Beloved." **Kalie, Kalley**

Kameko (Japanese) "Child of the tortoise."

Kamila (Arabic) "Perfect one." **Kamala, Kamilah, Kamillah**

Kara (Latin) "Dear one." **Cara, Karalee, Karrah**

Karen (Greek) "Pure one." Form of Catherine. Karen Black, actress; Karen Silkwood, U.S. atomic worker and activist. **Caren, Carin, Caron, Caryn, Karin, Karon, Karyn, Kerrin**

Karla (Old German) "A strong, country woman." Feminine form of Carl. **Carla, Karleen, Karlene, Karlie, Karline, Karly**

Katarina (Swedish) Form of Catherine or Katherine. Katarina Witt, Olympic figure skater. **Katerina, Katrina, Katrine**

Kate (Greek) "One who is pure." Short form of Katherine. Kate Capshaw, actress; Kate Smith, singer and actress; Kate Millett, feminist writer. **Cait, Caitlin, Caitrin, Katey, Katie, Katy**

Katherine (Greek) "Pure one." Katharine Hepburn, actress; Kathie Lee Gifford, TV talk show cohost; Kitty Carlisle, Kay Francis, and Katherine Ross, actresses; Katherine Mansfield, writer. **Karen, Kari, Kasia, Kassie, Kata, Katalin, Kate, Katerina, Katharine, Kathe, Kathi, Kathie, Kathleen, Kathryn, Kathy, Katie, Katinka, Katrien, Katrine, Katrinka, Katya, Kay, Kaye, Kit, Kitty**

Kayla Short form of Katherine. **Cayla, Kaela, Kaila**

Kayley (Irish Gaelic) "A descendant of the slender one. **Kaleigh, Kaley, Kayleigh, Kayly**

Keeley (Irish Gaelic) "Descendant of the white, slender one." Keely Smith, singer. **Kealey, Kealy, Keelie, Keelin, Keely, Kieli, Keighley, Kiley**

Kelly (Irish Gaelic) "Warlike one." (Old English) "From the wooded land." Kelly McGillis, actress. **Kelley, Kellen, Kellie**

Kelsey (Scandinavian) "From the island of ships." **Kelcey, Kelci, Kelcie, Kelcy, Kelsie, Kelsy, Kesley, Keslie**

Kendra (Old English) "Knowing one" or "from the hills." **Kendre, Kenna, Kinna**

Kenya (English) Name of the African country used as a first name.

Kerena (Hebrew) Biblical name meaning literally "animal's horn of eye-paint," referring to one with dark, attention-grabbing eyes. A shortened version of the biblical name Kerenhappuch, who was the third daughter of Job. **Keren**

Kerry (Irish Gaelic) "Dark-haired one," or the place name in Ireland. **Keri, Kerie, Kerrey, Kerri, Kerrian, Kerrie, Kiri**

Keziah (Hebrew) Biblical name from "cassia," which is a type of plant or shrub that grows in warm weather. Keshia Knight Pulliam, TV actress; Kizzy is a character in Alex Haley's *Roots*. **Keshia, Kesia, Kessiah, Kissiah, Kissie, Kissy, Kezia, Kizzie, Kizzy**

Kiara (Irish Gaelic) "Black-haired one." Feminine form of Kieran. **Kiaran, Kira**

Kim (Old English) "One who rules." Kim Basinger and Kim Novak, actresses. **Kym**

Kimberly (Old English) "From the ruler's clearing." **Kim, Kimba, Kimber, Kimberlee, Kimberleigh, Kimberley, Kimberlyn, Kimbley, Kimmie, Kimmy**

Kirsten (Danish) Form of Christine. **Chirstey, Ciorstiadh, Curstag, Kersten, Kicki, Kirstie, Kirstyn, Kyrstin**

Kristen (Latin) "Christian one." Form of Christine. Kristy McNichol, actress. **Krista, Kristan, Kristie, Kristin, Kristina, Kristine, Kristy, Krysten, Krystin**

Krystal (Greek) "Clear as ice." Krystal was the name of the likable matriarch on the TV show *Dynasty*. **Kristal, Krystle**

Kyle (Scottish Gaelic) "From near the narrow channel."
Kial, Kiley, Kyla, Kylie

Kyra (Greek) "Lordly one." Feminine form of Cyrus. Kiri
Te Kanawa, opera singer. **Kiri, Krene, Kyran**

■ PEN NAMES ■

Unlike actors and actresses who change their name in the hopes of enhancing their identity, writers usually change their name or adopt a "pen name" to conceal their identity. Women writers in particular have found pen names somewhat necessary. In days past, a woman often could not sell her writing to publishers, or customers—it was thought that no repectable woman would think of earning a living as an author.

Here are the names of eleven well-known writers and their *real* names.

REAL NAME	PEN NAME
Joan Aiken	Nicholas Dee
Anne Brontë	Acton Bell
Charlotte Brontë	Currer Bell
Emily Brontë	Ellis Bell
Mary Burke	Billie Burke
Janet Caldwell	Taylor Caldwell
Karen Dinesen	Isak Dinesen
Amandine Dudevant	George Sand
Mary Anne Evans	George Eliot
Marie de Flavigny	Daniel Stern
Harriet Beecher Stowe	Christopher Crowfield

Of course, there are as many reasons for a disguise as there are pen names, and many men also assumed a *nom de plume*. Here are a few celebrated examples:

REAL NAME	PEN NAME
Charles Lutwidge Dodgson	Lewis Carroll
Aleksei Peshkov	Maxime Gorky
Jean-Baptiste Poquelin	Molière
David John Moore Cornwall	John LeCarre
John Casey	Sean O'Casey
William Sydney Porter	O. Henry
Eric Arthur Blair	George Orwell
the crime-writing team of Frederic Dannay and Manfred Lee	Ellery Queen
Marie-Henri Beyle	Stendhal
Samuel Langhorne Clemens	Mark Twain

GIRLS
L

Lacey (French) "A young lady" or "lassy." Surname now used as a first name. **Lacie, Lacy**

Ladonna (French) "The lady of the house." The name is formed by the addition of the prefix La before Donna. **Ladonne, Ladonya**

Lakeisha (Arabic) "Womanly one." Modern U.S. name formed by the prefix La and the Arabic name Aiesha. **Lacrecia, Lakecia, Lakeesh, Lakesha, Lakeysha, Lakisha, Lakrisha**

Lalage (Greek) "One who is free to talk or babble." Name used by John Fowles in his novel *The French Lieutenant's Woman*. **Lalia, Lallie, Lally**

Lana (English) Short form of Helen or Alana. Lana Turner, actress. **Lanae, Lanette, Lanna, Lanny**

Lane (English) "From the little road." **Laina, Laine, Lanette, Laney, Lanie, Layne**

Lara (Latin) "Renowned one." Name of the heroine in Boris Pasternak's novel *Doctor Zhivago*. **Larisa, Larissa**

Larissa (Latin) "One who laughs cheerfully." **Lacey, Lara, Laryssa, Lissa**

Lark (English) "Larklike," referring to the cheerfulness and sweet song of the lark bird.

Latisha (Latin) "One who is happy." Modern form of Letitia. **Latasha**

Latonya (Latin) "Priceless one." Combination of the suffix La with a form of Antonia. **Latona, Latonia, Latoya**

Latrice (Latin) "Noble one." Combination of the suffix La with Patrice or Patricia. **Latricia, Latryce**

Laura, Lauren (Latin) "One with a laurel wreath," signifying a victory or an otherwise renowned person. Lauren Bacall, Laura Dern, and Lauren Hutton, actresses. **Lari,**

Laureen, Laurene, Laurie, Laurina, Lauryn, Lora, Loralie, Loreen, Loren, Loretta, Lorette, Lorie, Lorine, Lorna, Lorrie, Lorrin

Laurel (Latin) "Having qualities of the bay tree." **Laurie**

Lavender (Latin) "Like the herb," referring to the sweet smell of the lavender flower.

Laverne (Old French) "One who is springlike." One of the main characters on the TV show *Laverne and Shirley;* Laverne Andrews one of the Andrews Sisters. **Laverna, LaVerne, Lavina, Lavinia, Vern**

Lavinia (Latin) "Purified one." **Lavena, Lavina, Vinnie**

Leah (Hebrew) Biblical name meaning "weary one." Leah is the wife of Jacob. **Lea, Lee, Leigh, Lia, Liah**

Leala (Old French) "Faithful one." **Lealie**

Leandre (Greek) "One who is like a lioness." Feminine form of Leander. **Leanda, Leandra, Leanne, Leodora**

Leda (Greek) "Ladylike." In Greek mythology, Leda is a queen of Sparta who is raped by Zeus in the form of a swan and hatches two eggs, each containing sets of twins. **Leta, Lettitia**

Leigh (Old English) "From the open land, meadow, or clearing." Leigh Taylor Young and Lee Remick, actresses. **Lee**

Leila (Arabic) "Dark and intoxicating." **Laila, Layla, Leela, Leilah, Lela, Lelah, Lelia, Leyla**

Lena (Latin) "Alluring one." Lena Horne, entertainer. **Lenee, Leneta, Lenette, Lenita, Lina**

Lenora (Russian) Form of Eleanor. **Lenore, Leonora, Leonore, Nora, Norah**

Leona (Latin) "Like a lioness." Feminine form of Leo. Leontyne Price, opera singer. **Leola, Leone, Leonelle, Leontine, Leontyne**

Leslie (Scottish Gaelic) "From the meadow with the gray fortress." Leslie Caron, actress; Leslie Uggams, singer and actress. **Les, Lesley, Lesly, Lesslie, Lezlie**

Letitia (Latin) "One who is happy." Letitia Baldridge, etiquette expert. **Latashia, Latisha, Leda, Leta, Letice, Leticia, Letta, Lettice, Lettie, Letty, Tish**

Lexine (English) "One who helps others." Elaboration of Lexy. Form of Alexandra. **Lexene, Lexi**

Levana (Latin) "Of the dawn."

Levia (Hebrew) "To join." Feminine form of Levi. **Leana, Lia**

Liana (English) Form of Juliana or Gillian. **Leanne, Lian, Liane, Lianne**

Libby (English) Form of Elizabeth. **Lib, Libbey, Libbie, Liberty,**

Liesl (German) Form of Elizabeth. Name of one of the Von Trapp children in *The Sound of Music*. **Liesel, Lisel**

Lilac (Persian) "Bluish color," referring to the sweet-smelling lilac flowers.

Lilith (Hebrew) Biblical name meaning "evil spirit." Lilith is said to be the first wife of Adam, who was created separately from him. Because she did not obey him, she was turned into an ugly demon. Eve was then created out of Adam's rib so there would never be a question of Adam's authority. Lilith is thought to be the first feminist. **Lilly, Lily**

Lillian (Latin) "Like a lily flower." In Christianity, the lily symbolizes purity. Lillian Gish, actress; Lillian Hellman, writer; Lily Pulitzer, fashion designer; Lily Tomlin, actress and comedienne. **Lil, Lileana, Lili, Lilia, Lilian, Liliana, Lileana, Lilli, Lilly, Lily, Lilyan**

Linda (Spanish) "Beautiful." (Latin) "Tender, soft one." Linda Blair, Lynda Carter, and Linda Evans, actresses; Linda Ronstadt, singer. **Lin, Lindie, Lindy, Lyn, Lynda, Lynde, Lyndy, Lynn, Lynne**

Lindsay (Old English) "From the area of linden trees." Lindsay Wagner, actress. **Lindsey, Lindsie, Lindsy, Lindzy, Lynsay, Linsey**

Linette (Old French) "Like the linnet bird," referring probably to the bird's gracefulness. (Welsh) "An idol." Lynette is a character in the Arthurian legends much beloved by Gareth. **Lanette, Linet, Linetta, Linnet, Linnette, Lynette, Lynnet, Lynnette**

Linnea (Scandinavian) "Of the lime trees." **Linea, Lynea, Lynnea**

Lisa (English) "One whose allegiance is to God." Form of Elizabeth, although popular in its own right. **Leesa, Liesa, Lissa, Lisetta, Liz, Liza, Lizzie, Lizzy, Lys, Lyssa**

Liv (Scandinavian) "Full of life" or "protector." Liv Ullmann, actress.

Livia (Latin) "Olive branch," referring to the olive branch as a symbol of peace. Form of Olivia.

Liza (English) Form of Elizabeth. Liza Minnelli, entertainer. **Lizetta, Lizette, Lizzie, Lizzy**

Lois (Greek) Biblical name of Timothy's grandmother in the

New Testament. Possibly a form of Louise or Eloise. Lois Lane, character in *Superman*.

Lola (Spanish) "Strong woman of sorrows." Form of Dolores. Lola Montez, an Irish singer and dancer who so captivated Ludwig I, king of Bavaria, that she virtually ruled him and his country. **Lita, Lolita**

Lona (Middle English) "Solitary one." **Lonee, Loni, Lonna, Lonni, Lonnie**

Lorelei (German) "From the Rhine River."

Loretta (English) Form of Laura. Loretta Lynn, singer. **Lori, Lorie, Lorrie**

Lorraine (French) "From the Lorraine Province." (Old German) "From the territory of Lothar," and Lothar is defined as "the famous warrior." **Laraine, Lorain, Loraine, Lorane, Lorayne, Lorrain, Lorrayne**

Lotta (English) Short form of Charlotte. Lotte Lehmann, opera singer. **Lotte, Lotti, Lottie, Lotty**

Lotus (Greek) "Like the lotus flower."

Louise (Old German) "Famous battle maiden." Louisa M. Alcott, author of *Little Women;* Louise Nevelson, sculptor; Louella Parsons, Hollywood gossip columnist. **Lou, Louella, Louisa, Louisette, Lu, Luana, Luane, Luella, Luelle, Luisa, Luise, Lulu, Luwana**

Lucille, Lucy (Latin) "One who brings light." A name sometimes given to a child born at the break of day. Lucille Ball, actress; Lucy Stone, nineteenth-century feminist. **Lu, Lucetta, Lucette, Luci, Lucia, Luciana, Lucie, Lucienne, Lucilla, Lucina, Lucinda, Lucita**

Lucretia (Latin) "Rewarded with wealth." **Lucrece, Lucrecia**

Lunetta (Italian) "Little moonlike one." **Lunette**

Lydia (Greek) "A woman from Lydia," which is an area of Asia Minor. Lydia is the young sister in Jane Austen's *Pride and Prejudice*. **Lidi, Lidia, Lidiya, Lydie, Lyla**

Lynn (Old English) "From near the pool at the bottom of a waterfall." Lynn Fontanne and Lynn Redgrave, actresses. **Lin, Linn, Lyn, Lyndel, Lyndell, Lynette, Lynne, Lynnette**

Lyra (Greek) "Lyrical one." **Liris, Lyris**

GIRLS
M

Mabel (Old French) "Lovable, friendly one." From the Old French vocabulary word *amabel*. **Amabel, Mabelle, Mable, Mae, Maybel, Maybelle**

MacKenzie (Irish Gaelic) "Descended from the ruler." **Kenzie, Mackenzie**

Madeleine (Hebrew) Biblical name meaning "a woman from Magdala," a town near Galilee where St. Mary of Magdalene was born. Madeleine is the heroine of the children's story of the same name by Ludwig Bremelmans. Madeline Kahn, actress. **Dalenna, Lena, Lenna, Lina, Linn, Lynn, Lynne, Madalena, Madalyn, Maddi, Maddie, Maddy, Madelaine, Madelene, Madelina, Madeline, Madella, Madelle, Madlen, Madlin, Mady, Magdala, Magdalena, Malena, Marleagh, Marleen, Marlena, Maude, Maud**

Madge (English) "Pearl-like." Form of Margaret.

Madison (Old English) "Child of the brave warrior." **Maddie, Maddy**

Madonna (Latin) "My lady," referring originally to the Virgin Mary. Madonna Ciccone, American entertainer, has recently made it popular as a given name.

Maggie (English) Form of Margaret that has become popular as a name in its own right. Maggie Smith, English stage actress. **Mag, Maggee, Maggy**

Magnolia (Latin) "Like the beautiful magnolia blossom." **Mag, Maggy, Nola, Nolie, Noly**

Mahala (Hebrew) Biblical name meaning "tender one." Mahalia Jackson, singer. **Mahalah, Mahalia, Mahalah**

Maia (Greek) "One who tenderly nurses." In Greek mythology, Maia is the mother of Hermes, by Zeus. **Maiah, Maya, Mya**

Maida (Old English) "A young maiden." **Maddie, Maddy, Mady, Maidie, Maidy, Mayda**

Maisie (English) Form of Margaret. **Maisey, Maizey, Maysey, Mazey**

Mallory (Old German) "War counselor." (Old French) "Unfortunate or unlucky one." Currently popular for both boys and girls. **Mallorie, Malorie, Malory**

Malka (Hebrew) "Queenly one." **Malkah**

Malvina (Celtic) "Leader with a smooth brow or polished look." (Greek) "Thin, soft one." **Malva, Malvane, Malvy, Melva, Melvina**

Mamie (English) Form of Margaret or Mary. Name by which the wife of Dwight D. Eisenhower, thirty-fourth U.S. president, was known; Mamie Van Doren, actress, Name of main character in the play *Auntie Mame*. **Mame, Mamy, Mayme**

Mandy (English) "Lovable one." Form of Amanda or Miranda. **Manda, Mandie**

Manuela (Spanish) "God is with us." Feminine form of Emmanuel.

Mara (Hebrew) Biblical name meaning "bitter one." Naomi (pleasant one) requests to be called Mara, since the Lord has dealt bitterly with her. **Maraline, Mari**

Marcia, Marsha (Latin) "One belonging to or like Mars, the Roman god of war." Feminine form of Marcus. Marsha Mason, actress. **Marcela, Marcelle, Marcellina, Marcena, Marcene, Marci, Marcile, Marcina, Marcy, Marquita**

Margaret (Greek) "Pearl-like one." Margaret Smith Court, tennis player; Margaret Mitchell, author of *Gone With the Wind*; Margaret Thatcher, British prime minister. **Greta, Gretchen, Gretel, Madge, Maggie, Maisie, Margareta, Margarete, Margaretha, Margaretta, Margarette, Margarita, Marge, Margery, Marget, Margie, Margo, Margot, Marguerite, Marjorie, Majorie, Meg, Megan, Meghan, Meggie, Meggy, Peg, Peggy, Rita**

Margo (French) Form of Margaret. Margot Hemingway, actress and model. **Margaux, Margeaux, Margot**

Maria (Latin) Form of Mary. Maria Callas, opera singer; Maria Montessori, innovative educator; Maria Shriver, TV newscaster. Name of the heroines in both *West Side Story* and *The Sound of Music*. **Mari, Mariah, Marie, Mariel, Marietta**

Marian (Hebrew) "Rebellious one." (Old French) "A small Mary." Maid Marian, sweetheart of the legendary Robin

Hood. **Mariam, Mariana, Marianna, Marianne, Marion, Maryann, Maryanne**

Marigold (Old English) "Mary's gold," referring to the Virgin Mary. The flower so named has a golden color.

Marilyn Created out of combining Mary and Ellen or Mary and Lyn. Marilyn Horn, opera singer; Marilyn Monroe, actress. **Maralyne, Marilee, Marilene, Marrilyn, Marylin, Merilyn, Merrill**

Marina (Latin) "Warlike one." Feminine form of Marius, a Roman clan name or "from the sea." Princess Marina of Greece. **Marena, Marinna, Marna, Marni**

Marisa (Spanish) Elaboration of Maria. (Latin) "Of the sea." Marissa Berensen, model. **Mareesa, Maris, Marissa, Marris, Merrisa, Morissa**

Marjorie (English) Modern form of Margery or Margaret. This spelling could come from an association with the sweet-smelling herb marjoram. **Marge, Margery, Margie, Margy, Marje, Marjie, Marjory, Marjy**

Marlene (German) Form of Madeleine, Magdalena, or Magdalene. Marlee Matlin, actress; Marlene Dietrich, actress whose given name was Maria Magdalene von Losch. **Marlaina, Marlane, Marlee, Marleen, Marleene, Marlena, Marley, Marlie, Marline, Marna**

Martha (Arabic) Biblical name meaning "a lady." In the New Testament, when the sisters Mary and Martha receive a visit from Jesus, Mary sits at Jesus's feet, leaving Martha to do all the serving. As a result, the name is associated with one who does domestic work. Martha Washington, the First Lady of the U.S.; Martha Stewart, entertainer and author. **Marta, Martella, Marthe, Marti, Martie, Martita, Marty, Mattie, Matty, Pat, Patty**

Martina (Latin) "Woman warrior." Feminine form of Martin. Martina Navratilova, tennis player. **Mart, Marti, Marty, Tina**

Marva (Old French) "Miracle one." **Marvela, Marvella, Marvelle**

Mary Biblical name from Miriam and Marah. While the actual origin and meaning of this ever-popular name seems to remain a mystery, following are some of the traditionally espoused ones. (Latin) "Star of the sea." (Hebrew) "Bitter," referring to myrrh, the bitter incense used in biblical times, and "rebellious." Name of the Virgin Mary, mother of Jesus Christ. A popular name throughout the world. Mary Pickford, Mary Martin, and Mary Tyler Moore, actresses; Marla Maples, model. **Maire, Mame, Mamie, Manon, Mara,**

Marabel, Maria, Mariam, Marian, Marianna, Marianne, Mariel, Marietta, Marilee, Marilyn, Marin, Marion, Mariska, Marita, Maritsa, Marla, Marlo, Marya, Mary-ann, Maryanne, Maryellen, Marylou, Masha, Maura, Maureen, Maurene, Maurise, Mavra, Meriel, Merrill, Mimi, Minette, Minnie, Minny, Miriam, Mitzi, Moira, Moll, Mollie, Molly, Murial, Muriel, Murielle, Polly

Mathia (Hebrew) "A gift of God." Feminine form of Matthew. **Mathea, Mattea, Matthea, Matthia**

Matilda (Old German) "Mighty battle woman." Matilda was the wife of William the Conqueror. Also the name of Henry I of England's daughter. The name is known to schoolchildren through the song "Waltzing Matilda." **Maitilde, Mat, Matelda, Mathilda, Matilde, Mattie, Matty, Maud, Maude, Tilda, Tildy, Tillie, Tilly**

Maureen (Irish Gaelic) "A small Mary." (Old French) "Dark-complected." Feminine form of Maurice. Maureen Stapleton, actress. **Maura, Maurene, Maurine, Mo, Moira, Mora, Moreen, Morena**

Mauve (Latin) "One whose eyes are the color of lilac." **Maeve, Malva**

Mavis (Old French) "Like a song thrush." **Mave, Mayvis**

Maxine (Latin) "One of the greatest." Feminine form of Max. Maxene Andrews, one of the Andrews Sisters. **Max, Maxene, Maxi, Maxie, Maxy**

May (Latin) "Great one." (Hebrew) "Bitter." Form of Mary. Also, a month name referring to springtime. Mae West, actress; Maya Angelou, writer. **Mae, Mai, Maia, Maya, Maye**

Mead (Greek) "Honeywine." **Meade**

Meara (Irish Gaelic) "One who is merry and gay."

Megan (Welsh) "Like a pearl." Form of Margaret. Meg Ryan, actress. **Maegen, Meagan, Meaghen, Meg, Megen, Meggie, Meghan, Meghann**

Melanie (Greek) "Dark in complexion or clothing." Melanie Griffith, actress. **Malanie, Mel, Mela, Melantha, Melany, Mellie, Melly, Melonie, Melony, Milena**

Melba (Greek) "Soft, thin one." (Latin) "Like the mallow flower." Melba Moore, singer and actress. **Malva, Melva**

Melina (Greek) "Like honey" or "one with yellow-colored hair." **Meleana**

Melinda (Greek) "Sweet, like honey" and "tender, gentle

one." **Linda, Lindy, Linnie, Lynda, Malina, Malinda, Melynda, Mandy, Mindy**

Meliora (Latin) "To make better." **Melyora**

Melissa (Greek) "A honeybee," probably referring to the industriousness of the bee and the sweetness of the honey. Melissa Manchester, singer. **Lissa, Mel, Melessa, Melicent, Melisse, Melita, Mellie, Melly, Millicent, Millie, Milly, Missy**

■ HOW DOES THE NAME LOOK? ■

Americans are famous for respelling names. While some of us find a unique spelling to be distinctive, others are frustrated by the constant misspelling of their name. Only you can decide whether you want an Alice, Aliss, Alyce, Alys, or Alyss. Just make sure the spelling isn't so unusual as to change the way the name is pronounced.

Melody (Greek) "One who sings." **Melodie**

Mercedes (Spanish) "Merciful one." The name is taken from another title for the Virgin Mary, Santa Maria de las Mercedes (Our Lady of the Mercies). **Merci, Mercia, Mercy, Mersey**

Meredith (Old Welsh) "One of the Lord's magnificent leaders" and "a sea guardian." Originally a male name but now predominantly female. Meredith Baxter Birney, actress. **Meredithe, Meridath, Meridith, Merridie, Merridith, Merridy, Merry**

Meryl (Old French) "Like a blackbird." (Old Welsh) "Bright one from the sea." Meryl Streep, actress. **Merl, Merla, Merle, Merline, Merrill, Myrle, Myrlene**

Merry (Middle English) "One who is jolly and cheerful." **Merily, Merrie, Merrilee, Merrily**

Mia (Italian) "My or mine." A form of Michelle. Mia Farrow, actress.

Michelle (Hebrew) "One who strives to be like God." Feminine form of Michael. Michelle Pfeiffer, actress; "Michelle," Beatles song. **Mechelle, Micaela, Michaela, Michaelina, Michaeline, Michel, Michele, Micki, Mickie, Micky, Midge, Mikaela, Miquela, Misha**

Mignon (French) "Sweet, dainty, darling one." **Mignonette, Minette**

Mildred (Old English) "One who is strong in a gentle way." **Milley, Millie, Milly, Mindy**

Millicent (Old German) "Industrious, strong one." **Melicent, Mellisent, Melly, Milicent, Millie, Milly, Missie, Missy**

Mimi (Hebrew) "Rebellious one." Form of Miriam. Mimi is the heroine of Puccini's opera *La Bohème*. **Mimie**

Minerva (Latin) "Wise one." Minerva is the Roman goddess of wisdom. **Minivera, Minnie, Minny**

Mira (Latin) "Famous one." **Mirabel, Mirabell, Mirabella, Mirah, Mirella, Mirielle, Mirka, Myra**

Minna (Old German) "Tender affection." **Mina, Minette**

Miranda (Latin) "One who is admired." The name is said to have been invented by Shakespeare for the heroine of *The Tempest*. **Mandie, Mandy, Mindie, Mindy, Mira, Miran, Myra, Myranda, Randie, Randy**

Miriam (Hebrew) Biblical name meaning "bitter" or "rebellious." Miriam is Moses's older sister, a prophetess. The original form of the popular name Mary. **Mira, Miram, Mirra, Mirraim, Mirrian, Mitzi, Mitzie**

Misty (Old English) "From the mist." Heroine of the book and movie *Play Misty for Me*. **Misti**

Moira (Irish Gaelic) "Great one." Form of Mary. **Moyra**

Molly (Irish) Form of Mary. Molly Pitcher, American Revolutionary War heroine; Molly Ringwald, actress. **Mol, Mollie**

Mona (Irish Gaelic) "Nobel one." (Greek) "Single one." (Italian) "My lady." Mona Lisa, Da Vinci's famous painting. **Monah, Moyna**

Monica (Latin) "One who counsels wisely." (Greek) "Single one." St. Monica is the mother of St. Augustine; Mona Freeman, actress. Monica Seles, tennis player. **Mique, Mona, Moni, Monika, Monique**

Morgan (Old Welsh) "From the seashore" or "brilliant, famous one." Morgan Le Fay is the stepsister of the legendary King Arthur. Morgan Fairchild, actress. **Morgana, Morganne, Morgen**

Moselle (Hebrew) "Child rescued from the water." **Mozelle**

Muriel (Irish Gaelic) "One who is sea bright." (Arabic) "Bitter." (Middle English) "Merry one." Muriel Sparks, English writer. **Meriel, Murial, Murielle**

Musetta (Greek) "A source of inspiration." In classical Greek mythology, the Muses preside over music, poetry, and the arts. **Muse, Musette**

Myra (Greek) "Abundant." (Hebrew) "Bitter one," as in the incense myrrh. (Latin) "Admired one." Myra Hess, British pianist. **Mira, Mirah**

Myrna (Irish Gaelic) "Gentle, lovable one." Myrna Loy, actress. **Merna, Mirna, Moina, Morna, Moyna**

Myrtle (Greek) "The myrtle plant," which is the ancient Greek symbol of victory. **Mertle, Mirtle, Myrta, Myrtia**

GIRLS
N

Nadia (Russian) "Hopeful one." Nadia Comenici, Olympic gymnast; Nadine Gordimer, South African writer. **Nada, Nadeen, Nadine, Nadiya, Nady, Nadya, Nadzia, Natka**

Nancy (Hebrew) "Graceful one." Form of Anne that has become extremely popular in its own right. Nancy Lopez, golfer; Nancy Reagan, wife of fortieth U.S. president. **Nan, Nana, Nance, Nancey, Nancie, Nanette, Nanice, Nanine, Nannie, Nanny, Nanon, Nettie, Netty**

Naomi (Hebrew) Biblical name meaning "pleasant, delightful one." Naomi is the mother-in-law of Ruth and wife of Elimelech. **Naoma, Naomia, Naomie, Noami, Noemi**

Nastasia (Greek) "One who is resurrected." Form of Anastasia. Nastasia Kinski, actress.

Natalie (Latin) "Birthday of the Lord." A name given to girls born around Christmastime. Natalie Cole, singer; Natalia Makarova, ballerina; Natalie Wood, actress. **Nat, Nata, Natala, Natalia, Natalina, Nataline, Natalya, Nathalia, Natividad, Natty, Nettie, Netty, Talya**

Natasha (Russian) Form of Natalie. Often a nickname for Natalya. **Tasha**

Neila (Irish Gaelic) "A champion." Feminine form of Neil. **Neala, Neilla, Neille**

Nelia (Spanish) "Womanly." Short form of Cornelia. **Neile, Neilla, Nela, Nila**

Nell (English) "One of light." Short form of Eleanor. Nell Carter, singer. **Nellie, Nelly**

Nerissa (Greek) "Like a sea nymph." Nerissa is the clever lady-in-waiting who works for Portia in Shakespeare's *The Merchant of Venice*. **Nereida, Nerida, Nerina, Nerita**

Nerys (Modern Welsh) "Lordly one."

Nessa (Latin) "Pure one." Form of Agnes. (English) Short form of Vanessa. (Hebrew) "God's miracle." **Nasia, Nesia, Ness, Nessie, Neys**

Nettie (English) Short form of names such as Annette, Antoinette, or Jeannette but often used as a name on its own. **Netta, Netty**

Neva (Spanish) "Snowlike one." **Nevada, Neves, Nieves**

Ngaio (New Zealand) "One who words with wood." This is a type of tree in New Zealand used for building. Ngaio Marsh, mystery writer.

Nicole (Greek) "Of the victorious people." Feminine form of Nicholas. **Colette, Cosetta, Cosette, Nichol, Nichole, Nicki, Nickie, Nicky, Nicola, Nicoletta, Nicolette, Nicoli, Nicolina, Nicoline, Nicolle, Niki, Nikki**

Nina (Spanish) "Little girl." (Hebrew) "Graceful one." Form of Anne. (Russian) Short form of Antonina and Ninotchka. **Nena, Ninetta, Ninette, Ninon**

Noelle, Noëlle (Latin) "One born at Christmastime." **Noel, Noël, Noella, Noellyn**

Nola (Irish Gaelic) "Noblewoman." Feminine form of Nolan. **Nolana, Noleen**

Nona (Latin) "Ninth one." Name given to the ninth child born. **Nonah, Noni, Nonie, Nonna**

Nora (Greek) "One of light." Short form of Eleanor. (Latin) "Honorable one." Short form of Honoria. Nora is the main character in Henrik Ibsen's famous play *A Doll's House;* Nora Ephron, contemporary writer. **Norah, Noria, Norina, Norine**

Norma (Old German) "From the North." Feminine form of Norman. (Latin) "An ideal one." **Noreen, Normia**

Norris (Old French) "From the North" or "nurse." Norris Church Mailer, writer and wife of Norman Mailer. **Norice, Noris, Norrie**

Nova (Latin) "New one." A nice choice for someone from Nova Scotia. **Novia**

Nyssa (Greek) "One who begins." **Nissa, Nysa**

GIRLS
O

Octavia (Latin) "Eighth child." Feminine form of Octavius. Name of many women in the Roman imperial family. **Octavie, Ottavia, Tavia, Tavie, Tavy**

Odele (Greek) "A little ode or song." **Odelet, Odelette**

Odelia (Old English) "Prosperous one." (Hebrew) "One who praises God." **Odella, Odetta, Odette, Odilia, Othelia, Othilia, Uta**

Odessa (Greek) "From the long journey." Feminine form of Odysseus. It is also the name of a Russian city.

Olena (Russian) "One of light." Form of Helen. **Alena**

Olga (Russian) "Holy one." Feminine form of Oleg. Name of many of the women in the Russian imperial family. **Elga, Helga, Olenka, Olia, Olka, Olna, Olva, Olya**

Olivia (Latin) "Like an olive," which is the symbol of peace. Feminine form of Oliver. Olivia de Havilland, actress; Olivia Newton-John, singer. **Liva, Livia, Livvie, Nola, Nolita, Nollie, Olia, Olive, Olivette, Ollie, Olly, Olva**

Olwin (Welsh) "Pure, fair, blessed one." **Olwyn**

Olympia (Greek) "Heavenly one." The name refers to one from Mount Olympus, which is the home of the Greek gods. Olympia Dukakis, actress. **Olimpia, Olympe, Olympie**

Omega (Greek) "The last child" or "the end." Name of the last letter in the Greek alphabet.

Ona (Latin) "The one" or "united one." Oona Chaplin, wife of the comedian Charlie Chaplin. **Oona, Oonagh, Una**

Oneida (North American Indian) "Expected." **Onida**

Opal (Sanskrit) "Precious one, like the stone." **Opalina, Opaline**

Ophelia (Greek) "Serpentlike," referring to the serpent as the ancient symbol of immortality. Also (Greek) "Helpful one."

Ophelia is the name of the tragic heroine in Shakespeare's *Hamlet*. **Felia, Filia, Ofelia, Ofilia, Ophelie, Phelia**

Oprah (Hebrew) Biblical name meaning "fawnlike." In the Bible it is a male name, but now it is used predominantly by females. Oprah Winfrey, TV talk show host. **Ofra, Ophrah**

Oralie (Latin) "Golden one." Form of Aurelia. **Ora, Oriel, Oriola, Oriole, Orlena, Orlene**

Oriana (Latin) "One who rises." **Oriane**

Orla (Irish Gaelic) "A golden lady." A modern Irish name. **Orlagh**

Ornella (Italian) "From the flowering ash trees." **Ornetta, Ornette**

Oriole (Latin) "One with fair-colored hair." **Oralie, Oriel**

Ottilie (Old German) "Prosperous one." Feminine form of Otto. **Otilie, Ottolina, Ottoline, Otylia**

Owen (Latin) "Of noble birth." (Old Welsh) "Lamblike." Form of Evan. **Ewen**

GIRLS
P

Page (French) "A nobleman's servant." (Old English) "A child." **Paige**

Paloma (Spanish) "Dovelike," probably referring to the religious significance of the dove as a symbol for the Holy Spirit. Paloma Picasso, daughter of the artist Pablo Picasso.

Pamela (Greek) "Of all honey," referring to the sweetness of honey. Pamela is the heroine in Samuel Richardson's novel *Pamela*. **Pam, Pamella, Pammi, Pammie, Pammy**

Pandora (Greek) "Gifted one." In Greek mythology, Pandora opened the box containing all human evils as well as hope. **Doria**

Pansy (Old French) "One of thought." Also, the name of the flower. **Pansie**

Paris (Greek) "From the city in France." Originally a male name in classical Greek mythology. Paris is the man who carried off the beautiful Helene from Sparta to Troy and thus caused the Trojan War. Currently popular as a girl's name.

Patience (Latin) "One who suffers and endures." A Puritan virtue name quite popular among the Pilgrims.

Patricia (Latin) "A noblewoman." Feminine form of Patrick. Patsy Cline, country singer; Patty Duke, actress; Patti LaBelle, singer. **Pat, Patrica, Patrice, Patricio, Patrizia, Patsy, Patti, Pattie, Patty, Tricia, Trish, Trisha**

Paula (Latin) "Small one." Feminine form of Paul. Paula Abdul, singer; Pauline Porizkova, model. **Paolina, Pauleen, Paulene, Paulette, Paulina, Pauline, Paulyne, Pavla, Polly**

Pearl (Latin) "Pearl-like one" or "precious one." Pearl S. Buck, writer; Pearl Bailey, entertainer. **Pearla, Pearle, Pearline, Perl, Perle, Perry, Purly**

Peggy (English) Short form of Margaret from Meg. Peggy Ashcroft, English actress; Peggy Lee, singer. **Peg, Pegeen, Peggie, Peig, Peigi**

Pelagia (Greek) "From the open sea." **Pelage, Pelageya, Pelagie**

Penelope (Greek) "Like a bobbin," referring to the weaving and bobbing motion of the bobbin as it goes underneath the fabric on the loom. In Greek mythology, Penelope, the wife of Odysseus, spent time weaving and dodging the attentions of her many suitors during her husband's long absence. Penny Marshall, actress. **Pen, Penelopa, Penina, Penny**

Pepita (Spanish) "One who is fruitful." Form of Josephine. **Pepi, Peta, Pipi, Pippi**

Perdita (Latin) "Little lost one." Perdita is a character in Shakespeare's *The Winter's Tale* and in the Walt Disney movie *One Hundred and One Dalmatians*. **Perdie, Perdy**

Persephone (Greek) "Rebirth" or "of springtime." In Greek mythology, Persephone, the daughter of Zeus and Demeter, was abducted by Hades, god of the underworld, and forced to become his wife. So strong was her mother's grief that Persephone was permitted to return aboveground for four months each year, and her return marks the beginning of spring.

Persis (Greek) "From Persia." **Persa, Persia**

Petra (Greek) "Stonelike." Feminine form of Peter. **Pernilla, Pernille, Perrine, Pet, Peta, Petrice, Petrina, Petronella, Petronia, Pier, Pierette, Pietra**

Petula (Latin) "One who seeks" or "saucy one." Petula Clark, English singer. **Pet, Petunia**

Philadelphia (Greek) "Love of a kinsperson" or "brotherly love." Name of a city in the Bible as well as a city in the U.S. state of Pennsylvania. **Delphia, Delphie, Philly**

Philana (Greek) "Lover of men," referring to a woman who loves her husband. **Philene, Philina, Phillida, Phillidia**

Philippa (Greek) "A lover of horses." Feminine form of Philip. **Felipa, Filipa, Phil, Philipa, Philippe, Phillipine, Philly, Pippa, Pippy**

Philomena (Greek) "One who is well loved." **Filomena, Mena**

Phoebe (Greek) "Bright, shining one." In classical Greek mythology, Phoebe is another name for Artemis, goddess of the moon. Phoebe Cates, actress. **Phebe**

Phyllis (Greek) "One who is like foliage." In Greek mythology, Phyllis is a minor character who, lovesick, kills herself and turns into an almond tree. Phyllis Diller, comedienne; Phyllis George, former Miss America; Phyllis Whitney, writer. **Phillida, Phillis, Phylis, Phyllida, Phyllys**

Pia (Italian) "Pious one." Pia Zadora, entertainer.

Pierce (English) (Irish) "Rocklike one." Feminine form of Piers or Peter. **Pierette, Pierse**

Pilar (Spanish) "One who is a foundation or pillar," referring to a title of the Virgin Mary, Nuestra Señora del Pilar (Our Lady of the Pillar). **Pili, Pilita**

Piper (Old English) "A player of pipes." Piper Laurie, actress. **Pip**

Pippa (English) "A lover of horses." Short form of Philippa but used independently as well. Pippi Longstocking, popular children's character in books by Astrid Lindgren. **Pip, Pippi, Pippie, Pippy**

Placida (Latin) "Calm, serene one." **Placidia**

Polly (English) "Rebellious one." Form of Mary through Molly and similar to Meg and Peg. Polly is a character in the nursery Rhyme "Polly Put the Kettle On." Polly Bergen, actress. **Poll, Pollie, Pollyanna**

Pomona (Latin) "One who is fruitful."

Portia (Latin) "An offering." Feminine form of a Roman clan name, Porcius. Portia was the heroine of Shakespeare's *Merchant of Venice* and as a result has come to mean "a female lawyer." **Tia**

Posy (English) Short form of Josephine. Also associated with the vocabulary word referring to a bouquet of flowers. **Posey, Posie**

Prima (Latin) "The firstborn."

Primrose (Latin) "The first rose." It is also a flower in its own right, though not connected to the rose family. A name sometimes given to children born on Primrose Day, April 19.

Priscilla (Latin) "From a more primitive or ancient time." Priscilla Presley, wife of Elvis Presley. **Cilla, Pris, Prisca, Priscella, Prisilla, Prissie, Prissy**

Prudence (Latin) "Prudent one." A Puritan virtue name. **Pru, Prue, Pruddie, Prudy**

Prunella (Latin) "Plumlike." **Nel, Nella, Nellie, Nelly, Pru, Prue**

GIRLS
Q

Queenie (Old English) "Queenlike." **Queen, Queena, Queenette, Queeny**

Quenby (Scandinavian) "Womanly one."

Querida (Spanish) "Loved one."

Quiana (Modern American) "Graceful one." Form of Anna through Kiana. **Kia, Kiana, Quia, Quianna**

Quinta (Latin) "Fifth child." **Quinella, Quintana, Quintilla, Quintina, Quintona**

Quintessa (Latin) "The essence." **Tess, Tessa, Tessie**

GIRLS
R

Rachel (Hebrew) Biblical name meaning "lamblike." Rachel is the wife of Jacob and the mother (after being barren for years) of Joseph and Benjamin. Raquel Welch, actress. **Rachael, Rachele, Rachelle, Rae, Rahel, Rakel, Raquel, Ray, Raychell, Rey, Rochell, Rochelle, Shelley, Shelly**

Rae (Irish Gaelic) "One of grace." A shortened form of the surname MacRae, "son of grace." (Old English) "Doelike," which comes from a shortened form of the roe deer, who are known for their grace. **Raelene, Raelyn, Ralene, Ralina, Raline, Ralyn**

Raina (Russian) "Queenly." Form of Regina. (Old German) "Warrior woman." Feminine form of Rainer. **Raine, Ray, Rayna, Rayner**

Ramona (Spanish) "Wise and mighty protectress." Feminine form of Raymond. The *Ramona* books by Beverly Cleary. **Mona, Ramonda, Ramonde, Romona**

Rana (Arabic) "One who is beautiful to look at." **Ranya**

Randy (Old English) "Protectress." Feminine form of Randall or Randolph. (Latin) "Admirable one." Short form of Miranda. **Randa, Randene, Randey, Randi, Randie**

Rani (Sanskrit) "Queen." **Rajni, Rania, Ranice, Rayna**

Raphaela (Hebrew) "One who heals with God's guidance." **Rafa, Rafaela, Rafaelia, Raffaela**

Rebecca (Hebrew) Biblical name meaning "one who ties or joins together." Rebekah is the wife of Isaac and the mother of Esau and Jacob. *Rebecca* is the title of a popular novel by Daphne de Maurier. Rebecca DeMornay, actress; Rebecca West, novelist. **Becca, Becka, Becki, Beckie, Becky,**

Bekki, Reba, Rebeca, Rebecka, Rebekah, Rebekka, Rheba, Riva, Rivalee

Regan (Latin) "Royal, queenlike." Form of Regina. **Reagan**

Regina (Latin) "Queenly." **Gina, Regena, Reggie, Regiena, Regine, Reginia, Reina, Rina**

Reid (Old English) "Red-haired or ruddy-complected one." **Read, Reed**

Remy (French) "One from Rheims." **Remie**

Renata (Latin) "One who is reborn," referring to a spiritual rebirth. Renata Adler, writer; Renata Tebaldi, opera singer. **Reina, Renae, René, Renée, Renelle, Renie, Rennie**

Renée (Latin) Form of Renata popular in the United States. **Reenie**

Renita (Latin) "One who is firm," perhaps even "a resister." **Nita, René, Renie, Rennie**

Rhea (Greek) "Motherly one." In Greek mythology, Rhea is the mother of the gods, and wife and sister of Cronos. In Roman mythology, Rhea Silvia is the mother of Remus and Romulus, the founders of Rome. **Rea, Rhya, Ria**

Rhian (Welsh) "A royal maiden." **Rhiannon, Riane, Ryan**

Rhoda (Greek) "A rose." (Latin) "A woman from Rhodes" (known as the island of roses). The rose is considered to be the queen of flowers. *Rhoda* is the name of a TV show from the 1970s. **Rhodie, Rhody, Roda, Rodi, Rodina**

Rhona (Scottish Gaelic) "Strong, famous one." Feminine form of Ronald. Rona Barrett, Hollywood gossip reporter. **Roana, Rona**

Rhonda (Welsh) "From Rhondda Valley," a place in South Wales. **Ron, Ronnie, Ronny**

Richelle (Old German) "All-powerful one." Feminine form of Richard. **Rica, Ricarda, Ricca, Richarda, Richel, Richella, Richia, Richie, Richy, Ricki, Rickie, Ricky, Ritchie**

Riona (Irish Gaelic) "Queenly one."

Risa (Latin) "Filled with laughter." **Rissa**

Rita (Spanish) "Pearl-like." Short form of Margarita used as a given name in its own right. Rita Hayworth, actress. **Reeta, Rheta**

Riva (French) "From the riverbank." **Reeva**

Roberta (Old English) "Brilliant, famous one." Feminine

form of Robert. Roberta Flack, singer. **Bobbe, Bobbi, Bobbie, Bobby, Bobina, Bobine, Robbi, Robbie, Robby, Robenia, Robin, Robina, Robinia**

Robin (Old English) "Bright with fame." Form of Roberta. **Robbi, Robbie, Robbin, Robby, Robbyn, Robena, Robina, Robinett, Robinette, Robinia**

Rochelle (French) "From the little rock." **Rachelle, Rochele, Roshele, Shelley**

Roderica (Old German) "Infamous ruler." Feminine form of Roderick. **Roddie, Roddy**

Rolanda (Old German) "Famous across the land." Feminine form of Roland. **Orlanda, Rolande**

Rosa (Spanish) Form of Rose. Rosa Parks, civil rights activist; Rosa Ponselle, opera singer. **Rosanne, Rosella, Roselle, Rosetta, Rosette, Rosie, Rosina, Rosita, Rosy, Rozella**

Rosabel (Latin) "Beautiful rose." **Rosabele, Rosabella, Rosabelle**

Rosalie (French) Form of Rose. Possibly a combination of Rose and Lily. **Rosalee, Rosaleen, Rosalia, Rozalie**

Rosalind (Latin) "Lovely like a rose." Possibly a combination of Rose and Linda. Name of the heroine in Shakespeare's *As You Like It;* Rosalynn Carter, wife of thirty-ninth U.S. president; Rosalind Russell, actress. **Rosalinda, Rosaline, Rosalyn, Rosalynd, Rosalynn, Roseline, Roslyn, Roz, Rozalin**

Rosamond (Old German) "Famous protecting one." (Latin) "Rose of the world" and "like a pure rose." **Rosamonde, Rosamund, Rosamunda, Rosemonde, Rozamund**

Rosanne (English) "Graceful like the rose." Rosanne Arquette, actress. Combination of Rose and Anne. **Roanna, Roanne, Rosan, Rosanna, Roseanne, Rozanne**

Rosemary (Latin) "Like the dew from the sea," referring to the look of the herb. Also can be interpreted as a combination of Rose and Mary. **Rosemaria, Rosemarie, Rosie**

Rowena (Old English) "A friend known throughout the land." (Celtic) "White-haired one." **Ranna, Rena, Ro, Ronnie, Ronny, Row, Rowe**

Roxanne (Persian) "Dawnlike." Name of the wife of Alexander the Great; heroine in Edmond Rostand's well-known tale *Cyrano de Bergerac;* Roxanne Pulitzer, writer and ex-wife of Peter Pulitzer. **Roxane, Roxann, Roxanna, Roxene, Roxi, Roxie, Roxine, Roxy**

Ruby (Latin) "Red," referring to the ruby, a precious stone. Ruby Dee, actress. **Rubi, Rubie, Rubye**

Rufina (Latin) "Red-haired one." Feminine form of Rufus.

Ruth (Hebrew) Biblical name meaning "a compassionate friend" or "a companion." The biblical Ruth left her homeland to be with her mother-in-law, Naomi. Ruth Gordon, actress. **Ruthe, Ruthi, Ruthie**

Ruthann (Hebrew) "A graceful friend." Combination of Ruth and Ann. **Ruthanne**

GIRLS
S

Sabina (Latin) "From Sabine." The Sabines were an ancient tribe in Italy who were raided by the Romans. Legend has it that the Romans made off with a great many of the Sabine women, causing war to ensue. **Bina, Saba, Sabin, Sabine, Savina**

Sabrina (Latin) "From the border or boundary line." **Brina, Sabra, Zabra, Zabrina**

Sadie (Hebrew) "Princess." Form of Sarah used as a given name in its own right. **Sada, Sadye, Saidy**

Sage (Latin) "Knowing one."

Saffron (English) "One with the coloring of saffron," referring to the yellowy-orange color of the spice.

Salena (Latin) "From the salt." **Salina**

Sally (Hebrew) "Princess." Form of Sarah used as a given name in its own right. Sally Field and Sally Struthers, actresses; Sally Ride, astronaut. **Sal, Sallie, Sallyann**

Salome (Hebrew) Biblical name meaning "peaceful one." Salome is the stepdaughter of King Herod. Oscar Wilde wrote a play about her titled *Salome*. **Saloma, Salomi**

Salus (Latin) "Salvation." **Salas, Salud**

Samantha (Aramaic) "One who listens." (Hebrew) "One whose prayers God has listened to." Feminine form of Samuel. Samantha Stevens is the witch on the TV show *Bewitched,* which began airing in 1964. **Sam, Samella, Samelle, Sammie, Sammy, Samuela, Samuelle**

Samara (Hebrew) "From Samaria" or "ruled by God," referring to those living in the Palestinian city of Samaria. **Samaria**

Sancia (Latin) "Holy, sacred one." **Sancha, Sanchia, Sancie, Sancy**

Sandra (Greek) "One who helps mankind." Short form of Alexandra. Sandra Dee, actress; Sandra Day O'Connor, first female U.S. Supreme Court justice. **Sandi, Sandie, Sandy, Saundra, Zandra**

Sapphire (Greek) "One with blue-colored eyes like the precious stone." **Saphira, Sapphira, Sephira**

Sarah (Hebrew) Biblical name meaning "princess." The wife of Abraham and mother of Isaac. Sarah Bernhardt and Sarah Miles, actresses. **Sadie, Sadye, Sal, Sallie, Sally, Sara, Sarai, Sarena, Sarene, Sarette, Sari, Sarie, Sarine, Sarita, Sayre, Serita, Shara, Shari, Sharon, Sheree, Sheri, Sherie, Sorcha, Zara, Zarah**

Sasha (Russian) Form of Alexandria. **Sacha, Sascha**

Saskia (Dutch) "Of Saxon extraction." Name of the wife of the Dutch painter Rembrandt.

Savannah (Spanish) "From the open land." Also, the name of a U.S. city in Georgia. **Savanna**

Scarlett (Middle English) "Having scarlet coloring." The name of the heroine in Margaret Mitchell's *Gone With the Wind* and title of the sequel to it by Alexandra Ripley. **Scarlet**

Sebastiana (Latin) "Well-respected one." Feminine form of Sebastian. **Seb, Sebastiane**

Selena (Greek) "Of the moon." Another name for the Greek goddess of the moon. **Celene, Celine, Lena, Lina, Salena, Salina, Selina, Seline**

Selma (Old German) "Divine warrior." Feminine form of Anselm. (Irish Gaelic) "Fair one." **Zelma**

Septima (Latin) "Seventh one."

Seraphina (Hebrew) "Ardent one." Seraphim are an order of angels who stand in the presence of God. **Sera, Serafina, Seraphine**

Serena (Latin) "Calm one." **Sereena, Serenna, Serina**

Shaina (Hebrew) "Beautiful one." Shana Alexander, writer. **Shaine, Shane, Shanee, Shanie, Shayna, Shayne**

Shannon (Irish Gaelic) "Old, wise one." Name of a river in Ireland. **Channa, Shana, Shanna, Shannan, Shannen, Shanon, Shauna, Shawna**

Sharon (Hebrew) Biblical place name "from the open plain." Biblical references include "the rose of Sharon," refering perhaps to an open plain full of beautiful roses. **Shara, Sharene, Shari, Sharona, Sharone, Sharron, Sharyn, Sherri, Sherry, Sherye**

Shauna (Irish) "Gracious one." Feminine form of John. **Sean, Seana, Shaun, Shawn, Shawna, Siana, Sianna**

Sheba (Hebrew) "From Sheba." Short form of Bathsheba. **Saba, Sheva**

Sheena (Scottish Gaelic) "Gracious one." Form of Jane. Sheena Easton, singer. **Sheenagh, Sheenah, Shena**

Sheila (Irish Gaelic) "Blind one." Form of Cecilia. **Selia, Sheela, Sheilah, Shela, Shelagh, Shelia, Sheyla**

Shelby (Old English) "From the estate on the edge of the hillside." **Shelbi, Shelly**

Shelley (Old English) "From the meadow on the edge of the hillside." Shelley Winters, Shelley Duvall, and Shelley Long, actresses. **Shell, Shellie, Shelly**

Sherry (French) "Dear one." Phonetic spelling of Cherie. Probably an additional influence is the name of the wine. **Sheree, Sheri, Sherie, Sherri, Sherye**

Shirley (Old English) "From the bright clearing." Shirley Jones and Shirley MacLaine, actresses; Shirley Temple Black, actress and ambassador. **Sherley, Sheryl, Shir, Shirl, Shirlee, Shirleen, Shirlene, Shirlie, Shirly**

Shulamite (Hebrew) "Peaceful one." A form of the Hebrew word *shalom*. **Shula, Shulamit, Shulamith**

Sibyl (Greek) "A prophetess." **Cybil, Cybill, Sib, Sibella, Sibille, Sibyll, Sybil, Sybilla, Sybille**

Sidonia (Latin) "A woman from Sidon." **Sidonie, Sidony**

Sigourney (Scandinavian) "New and victorious." Sigourney Weaver, actress. **Signe, Signi, Signy**

Sigrid (Scandinavian) "Beautiful, victorious counselor." **Sigy, Siri**

Sigrun (Scandinavian) "Victorious and secretive one."

Simone (Hebrew) "One who listens respectfully." Feminine form of Simon. Simone de Beauvoir, French writer. **Simmie, Simona, Simonette, Simonne**

Sirena (Greek) "One with enchanting song." In Greek mythology, the Sirens lured sailors to their island with their irresistible song and so enchanted them that they were unable to leave and died of hunger.

Sissy (Latin) "One who has difficulty seeing." Form of Cecilia. Also, a nickname for "sister." Sissy Spacek, actress.

Sonia (Russian) Form of Sophia. Sonja Henie, figure skater. **Sonja, Sonnie, Sonny, Sonya, Sunny**

Sophia (Greek) "Wise one." Sophia Loren, Italian actress;

Sophia Smith, founder of Smith College. **Sofia, Sofie, Sonia, Sonny, Sonya, Sophey, Sophi, Sophie, Sunny**

Sophronia (Greek) "Sensible, prudent one." **Sofrona, Sofronia**

Sorrel (Old French) "One with reddish-brown hair." Also, the name of a plant. **Sorel, Sorella**

Stacy (Greek) "One who is reborn." Short form of Anastasia. **Stace, Stacey, Stacia, Stacie, Stasia**

Stella (Latin) "Starlike." Name of a character in Tennessee Williams's famous play *A Streetcar Named Desire*. **Estelle, Star, Starla, Starr, Stelle**

Stephanie (Greek) "One who is crowned." Feminine form of Stephen. Princess Stephanie of Monaco; Stefanie Powers, actress; Stevie Nicks, singer; Steffi Graf, tennis player. **Stefa, Stefanie, Steffi, Steffie, Stepha, Stephani, Stephannie, Stephenie, Stephi, Stephie, Stevana, Stevanna, Stevena, Stevie**

Stockard (Old English) "From near the hardy tree stump." Stockard Channing, actress.

Susan (Hebrew) "Lilylike" referring to the innocence and purity of a lily. Susan B. Anthony, American reformer; Susan Hayward, Susan Sarandon, actresses. **Sue, Sukey, Suki, Susana, Susette, Susi, Susie, Susy, Suzi, Suzie, Suzy, Suzzy, Zsa Zsa**

Susanna (Hebrew) Biblical name meaning "lily." Susanna was falsely accused of adultery by her husband, Joachim. It is thanks to the wisdom of Daniel that her lily-white reputation was restored. Suzanne Pleshette and Suzanne Somers, actresses. **Sanna, Susana, Susannah, Susanne, Susette, Suzanna, Suzanne, Suzette, Zuzanna**

Swoosie (American) "Half swan, half goose." Swoosie Kurtz, actress.

Sydney (Old English) "From the meadow by the river." (Old French) "From the town of St. Denis." Feminine form of Sidney. Sydney Biddle Barrows, author of *The Mayflower Madam*. **Syd, Sydel, Sydelle**

Sylvia (Latin) "A maiden from the forest." Sylvia Porter, financial writer; Sylvia Plath, American poet. **Silva, Silvana, Silvia, Silvie, Sylvana, Zilvia**

GIRLS
T

Tabitha (Aramaic) "Gazellelike," referring to the bird's swift grace and lustrous eyes. Tabatha is the name of Samantha's daughter on the TV series *Bewitched*. **Tabatha, Tabbi, Tabbie, Tabbitha, Tabby, Tabita**

Tace (Latin) "Silent one." **Tacey, Tacita, Tacy**

Talitha (Aramaic) "Young maiden." **Taletha, Talicia, Talisha, Talita**

Tallulah (American Indian) "Running or leaping water." Tallulah Bankhead, actress. **Tallie, Tallou, Tallow, Tally, Talula**

Tama (American Indian) "A thunderbolt." **Taima**

Tamar (Hebrew) Biblical name meaning "palm tree," referring to the tree's beauty and grace. Tammy Wynette, country singer. **Tama, Tamara, Tamarah, Tammie, Tammy, Tamour, Tamra, Thamar**

Tania (Russian) "Fairy queenlike." Short form of Tatiana. Tanya Tucker, country singer. **Tana, Tanja, Tanya, Tati**

Tanisha (American) Unknown origin, though it is often given to children born on Monday. **Taneisha, Tanesha, Taneshia, Tanish, Tenesha, Teniesha, Tenisha**

Tansy (Greek) "Immortal one." **Tandi, Tandy**

Tara (Irish Gaelic) "From the rocky hill." Name of a town in Ireland with a large castle that is said to be the home of many ancient Irish kings. Also, the name of the O'Hara family estate in *Gone With the Wind*. **Tarah, Tarra, Tarrah, Taryn, Terra**

Tasha (Russian) "Christmastime." Short form of Natasha used as a given name in its own right. **Tashia, Tassia**

Tate (Old English) "Cheerful one." **Taite, Tayte**

Tatiana (Russian) "Fairy queen" or "giant one." **Tania, Tanya, Tati, Tatiania, Tawnya**

Tatum (English) "One who brings good cheer." Tatum O'Neal, actress. **Tate, Tayt, Taytum**

■ IS VIRGINIA A PERSON A PLACE . . . OR BOTH? ■

In America, among the many freedoms we enjoy is the right to name our children anything we like. In France, Germany, and Sweden, courts have jurisdiction over names, and a magistrate can refuse to allow a name that the courts deem unseemly.

And so, in America, there are children named "God" and "Chastity." In Wisconsin last year a "Colt," a "Fuzzy," and a "Whisper" were born. One new trend that is gaining popularity is the use of geographical names. Some of these are purely jingoistic. For example, in Alabama, "Bama" has become a common name. In Washington, D.C., Paris has become a popular girl's name. One young couple recently contemplated changing their daughter's name to "Budapest" from "Paris" when they found out that their original choice wasn't so original after all.

If you want to join the geographical-name movement, the following is a list of place names that might appeal:

Asia	Melbourne
Austin	Paris
Capri	Persia
Chelsea	Philadelphia
Cheyenne	Phoenix
China	Reno
Cleveland	Rome
Dakota	Savannah
Denver	Stanford
Holland	Vienna
India	Verona
Kenya	

Tawny (Middle English) "One with a warm, sandy coloring," or "well tanned." **Tawney**

Taylor (Middle English) "A tailor." Taylor Caldwell, writer. **Tay**

Temperance (Latin) "One who is moderate." A Puritan virtue name.

Tempest (Old French) "Stormy one." **Tempestine**

Tertia (Latin) "Third one." **Tercia, Terza**

Tessa (Greek) "Fourth one." Heroine in Thomas Hardy's *Tess of the D'Urbervilles*. **Tess, Tessie, Tessy**

Thadine (Greek) "Given by God." (Hebrew) "Praised one." Feminine form of Thaddeus. **Thada, Thadda, Thaddea**

Thalassa (Greek) "She who comes from the sea."

Thalia (Greek) "One who grows and blooms." In Greek mythology, Thalia is the Muse of comedy and also one of the Graces known for rejoicing.

Thelma (Greek) "One who is willed or wished for." Heroine of Marie Corelli's novel *Thelma;* Thelma Ritter, actress.

Theodora (Greek) "A gift from God." Feminine form of Theodore. **Dora, Fedora, Feodora, Teddi, Teddie, Teddy, Teodora, Theda, Theo, Theodisia, Theodoria**

Theophilia (Greek) "Loved by God."

Theresa possibly (Greek) "From the harvest or bounty." St. Teresa of Avila, a sixteenth-century Spanish nun. Mother Teresa, missionary nun; Terri Garr, actress. **Tera, Tere, Teresa, Terese, Teresita, Teressa, Teri, Terri, Terrie, Terry, Terrye, Terza, Tess, Tessa, Tessie, Tessy, Thera, Therese, Theresia, Tracie, Tracy, Tresa, Trescha, Tressa, Zita**

Thirza (Hebrew) "Pleasant, delightful one." **Thersa, Thersea, Therza, Tirza**

Thomasina (Hebrew) "Twinlike." Feminine form of Thomas. **Tamasin, Tamasine, Tamsin, Tamsyn, Thomasa, Thomasin, Thomasine, Thomazin, Tomasina**

Thora (Scandinavian) "Thunderlike." Feminine form of Thor. **Thyra, Tyra**

Tia (Spanish) "An aunt." Also, a short form of Letitia. **Tita**

Tiara (Greek) "One with a jeweled headress." **Tia, Tiana**

Tierney (Irish Gaelic) "Child of the lordly one." **Tieran, Tierany**

Tiffany (Greek) "God appears." Originally a name given to girls born on the Epiphany (January 6). Now it is associated with the name of the fashionable New York jewelry store.

Tiffaney, Tiffani, Tiffanie, Tiffiney, Tiffini, Tiffiny, Tiffy, Tiphani

Tilda (Old German) "Victorious one." Short form of Matilda. Tilly Olsen, writer. **Tildie, Tildy, Tillie, Tilly**

Tina Short form of Christina and other names ending in "tina" or "tine." Now commonly used as a given name in its own right. Tina Brown, editor of *Vanity Fair* magazine; Tina Turner, singer. **Teena, Tiena**

Tirion (Modern Welsh) "Gentle, kind one."

Toby (Hebrew) "From the goodness of God." Tovah Feldshuh, Broadway actress. **Tobey, Tobi, Tova, Tovah, Tove**

Toni (Latin) "So special that she is beyond price." Short form of Antonia. Toni Morrison, U.S. novelist. **Toinette, Toni, Tonia, Tonie, Tony, Tonya**

Topaz (Greek) "The gemstone topaz."

Tory (Latin) "Victorious one." Short form of Victoria used as a given name in its own right. **Torey, Tori, Torie, Torrie**

Tracy (Irish Gaelic) "Brave one." (Greek) "Of the harvest." Short form of Theresa. Tracy Lord, heiress played by Katharine Hepburn in the movie *The Philadelphia Story*. Tracy Austin, tennis player. **Tracee, Tracey, Tracie**

Trina (Greek) "Pure one." Short form of Katherine and Katrina. **Treena, Trinette**

Trinity (Latin) "A triad," referring to the Holy Trinity. **Trini, Trinidad**

Trisha (Latin) "Noble one." Short form of Patricia. **Tricia, Trish**

Trista (Latin) "Sad or melancholy one."

Trixie (Latin) "One who brings joy." Form of Beatrix. **Tressie, Trixi, Trixy**

Trudy (Old German) "Loved one." A short form of Gertrude. **Trude, Trudey, Trudie**

Tuesday (Old English) "One born on Tuesday." Tuesday Weld, actress.

Twyla (English) Possibly "two threads woven together" or "an abbreviation of twilight." Twyla Tharpe, dance choreographer. **Twila**

Tyne (Old English) "River." Tyne Daly, actress.

GIRLS
U

Udele (Old German) "Fortunate, prosperous one." **Uda, Udo, Ute**

Ulrika (Old German) "One with a large estate" or "from the family of the ruler." Feminine form of Ulrich. **Eula, Ula, Ulla, Ulrica, Ulrike, Rica, Rikka**

Ultima (Latin) "One who is reserved or aloof."

Una (Latin) "The one" or "from a unified whole." (Irish Gaelic) "Lamblike." Name of a character in Edmund Spenser's *The Faerie Queene*. **Ona, Oona, Oonagh**

Undine (Latin) "From the waves."

Unity (Latin) "A unified one."

Uriel (Hebrew) Biblical name meaning "of the light of God." Feminine form of Uriah held by two minor characters in the Bible. **Urial, Urice**

Ursula (Latin) "Like a young she-bear." Name of one of the sisters in D. H. Lawrence's novel *Women in Love*. Ursula LeGuin, writer. **Sula, Ursa, Ursala, Ursie, Ursule, Ursulina, Ursuline, Ursy**

GIRLS
V

Valda (Scandinavian) "Renowned ruler." Feminine form of Valdemar. **Valdis, Velda**

Valentine (Latin) "Strong, healthy one." **Val, Valencia, Valentia, Valentina, Velora**

Valerie (Latin) "One who is strong." Feminine form of a Latin clan name. Valerie Harper, actress. **Val, Valarie, Valeria, Valeriana, Valery, Valeska, Valetta, Valia**

Valeska (Russian) "Illustrious ruler."

Valonia (Latin) "From the vale."

Vanessa (Greek) "Butterflylike." Vanessa Redgrave, actress; Vanessa Williams, Miss America. **Esther, Van, Vanesa, Vanetta, Vania, Vanna, Vannie, Vanny**

Vega (Arabic) "One who is like a bright star."

Velma Possibly (Old German) "A determined guardian." Form of Wilhelmina. **Vilma**

Velvet (Middle English) "One who is soft like fleece." **Velvina, Velvor**

Venetia (Latin) "From Venice." **Venezia, Venecia, Venice, Venise, Vennice**

Venus (Latin) "Lovely one." Venus is the Roman goddess of beauty and love. **Venita, Vinita, Vinnie, Vinny**

Vera (Latin) "One who is true." (Russian) "Faithful one." Vera Miles, actress. **Vere, Verena, Verene, Verina, Verine**

Verena (Old German) "One who defends and protects." **Verneta, Vernita, Virina**

Verity (Latin) "True one." A Puritan virtue name. **Verita, Veritie**

Verna (Latin) "Springlike." Feminine form of Vernon. Verna Felton, actress. **Vern, Vernal, Verne, Vernetta, Vernis, Virna**

Verona (Italian) "One from Verona." **Veron, Veronica**

Veronica (Latin) "A true image," referring to the legend of St. Veronica in which Christ left an image of his face on the cloth Veronica gave him to wipe his face with en route to his crucifixion. **Ronica, Ronnie, Ronny, Vera, Veronice, Veronika, Veronike, Veronique**

Vesta (Latin) "One who guards the fire." The name of the Roman goddess of the hearth and home. **Vessy, Vest**

Victoria (Latin) "Victorious one." Victoria, Queen of England; Victoria Principal, actress. **Viccy, Vicki, Vickie, Vicky, Vikki, Vikky, Viktoria, Vitoria, Vittoria**

Vignette (French) "Little, vinelike one." **Vignetta**

Vina (Spanish) "Of the vineyard."

Violet (Latin) "Like the violet flower." **Iolatha, Viola, Violante, Violetta, Violette, Yolanda, Yolanthe**

Virginia (Latin) "A virginal young maiden." Probably influenced by the astrological sign Virgo. Virginia Woolf, English writer. **Ginger, Ginnie, Ginny, Jinnie, Jinny, Virgie, Virginie, Virgy**

Vita (Hebrew) "Beloved one." (Latin) "Life." Vita Sackville-West, English writer. **Veda, Veta, Vitia**

Vivian (Latin) "One who is alive or lively." (Irish Gaelic) "A white maiden." Vivien Leigh, actress. **Viv, Viva, Vivi, Viviana, Viviane, Vivie, Vivien, Vivienne, Vivyian**

Voleta (Old French) "One with a flowing veil." **Volet, Voletta**

GIRLS
W

Walda (Old German) "Famous ruler." Feminine form of Waldamar. **Welda**

Wallis (Old English) "From Wales." Feminine form of Wallace. Wallis Warfield Simpson, duchess of Windsor. **Walli, Wallie, Wally**

Wanda (Old German) "Wandering one." **Wandie, Wandis, Wenda, Wende, Wendie, Wendy**

Wanetta (Old English) "Fair, pale one." **Wynetta**

Wendy (Old German) "One who wanders." Feminine form of Wendell. Wendy is a much-loved character in J. M. Barrie's story *Peter Pan*. **Wende, Wendeline, Wendelle, Wendi, Wendie, Wendye**

Wenona (American Indian) "Firstborn girl." Winona Ryder, actress. **Wenonah, Winona, Wynona**

Wesley (Old English) "From the western valley." **Lee, Leigh, Wellesley, Wes, Wesly**

Whitney (Old English) "From near the white island." Whitney Houston, singer.

Wiara (Polish) "One who is true and faithful." **Wiera**

Wilfreda (Old German) "One who wants peace." **Freddie, Freddy, Wilfy, Willie, Willy**

Willow (English) "Thin and graceful," referring to the willow tree.

Wilma (Old German) "A firm guardian." Short form of Wilhelmina, which is a feminine form of William. Wilhelmina, queen of the Netherlands; Willa Cather, writer; Wilma Flintstone, character in the Hanna-Barbera comic strip and TV series *The Flintstones*. **Mina, Minna, Minni, Minnie, Minny, Vilhelmina, Wilhelma, Willa, Willabelle, Willamina, Willetta, Willette, Willie, Willmetia, Willy, Wilmette, Wylamina, Wylma**

Winnifred (Old German) "A peace-loving friend." (Welsh) "Fair one." Form of Guinevere. **Freda, Freddi, Freddie, Freddy, Winifred, Winne, Winnie, Winny, Wynn, Wynnie**

Wynne (Old English) "A friend." (Old Welsh) "White, fair-skinned one." **Winnie, Winny, Wyn, Wynn, Wynnie**

GIRLS
XYZ

Xanthe (Greek) "One with hair of golden yellow." **Xantha**

Xaviera (Arabic) "Bright, brilliant one." (Spanish) "Owner of the new household." Feminine form of Xavier. Xaviera Hollander, the "happy hooker." **Zaviera**

Xenia (Greek) "One who is hospitable, especially to strangers." **Xena, Zena, Zenia, Zina**

Xylona (Greek) "One from the forest." **Xylene, Xylia, Xylina**

Yael (Hebrew) Biblical name meaning "like a wild she-goat." **Jael**

Yaffa (Hebrew) "Beautiful one." **Jaffa, Yafit**

Yasmin (Arabic) "Like the small, white jasmine flower." **Yasmeen, Yasmina**

Yehudit (Modern Hebrew) "From Judea." Form of Judith. **Yahuda**

Yelena (Russian) "Of the light." Form of Helen.

Yente (Hebrew) "Kind one," though it has come to denote a gossipy woman.

Yo (Japanese) "Good" or "positive." Yoko Ono, artistic wife of John Lennon. **Yoko**

Yolanda (Greek) "Like a violet flower." **Iolanthe, Jolan, Jolantha, Yalinda, Yalonda, Ylonda, Yolande, Yolonda, Youlanda**

Yseult (Welsh) "Fair one." **Ysanne, Ysolde**

Yusra (Arabic) "Affluent one." **Yusriyya**

Yvonne (French) "A little archer." Feminine form of Yves. **Evonne, Iva, Ivona, Ivonne, Nonna, Vonnie, Yvette, Yvona**

Zahava (Modern Hebrew) "Golden one." **Zahavah**

Zakiyya (Arabic) "Virtuous, pure one." **Zakia**

Zara (Arabic) "Bright like the dawn." (Hebrew) "Blossoming one." Name given to Princess Anne's daughter. **Zahra, Zarah, Zaria, Zuhayr, Zuhra**

Zaynab (Arabic) "A lovely fragrant plant." A popular Arab name. **Zainab**

Zelda (Old German) "Battle maiden." Form of Griselda. (Yiddish) "One of good fortune." Zelda Fitzgerald, flamboyant wife of American writer F. Scott Fitzgerald. **Zelde**

Zella (Greek) "Possessing zeal." **Zelia, Zelie, Zelina**

Zenia (Greek) "Charitable, hospitable one." **Xenia, Zeni, Zina**

Zenobia (Greek) "Giver of life." Zenobia was a third-century queen of Palmyra. **Zena, Zenda, Zenina, Zinovia**

Zinnia (Latin) "The zinnia flower." **Zinia**

Zipporah (Hebrew) Biblical name meaning "birdlike." The name of Moses's wife. **Ziporah, Zippora, Ziproh**

Zoe (Greek) "Life." Zoe Caldwell, actress. **Zoee, Zoey, Zoie, Zowie**

Zofia (Polish) "Wise one." Form of Sophia. **Zifuam Zosia, Zsofia**

Zola (Italian) "A little ball of earth."

Zona (Greek) "Girdlelike." Zona Gale, Pulitzer Prize-winning writer.

Zsa Zsa (Hungarian) "Lily white." Form of Susan. Zsa Zsa Gabor, actress.

Zula (English) "From the Zulu people," a tribe in southern Africa.

If you enjoyed *Choose The Perfect Name for Your Baby*, then look for these other Longmeadow Press titles:

ITEM No.	TITLE	PRICE
0681410337	*Father And Child* by Carolyn T. Chubet	$14.95
0681404515	*No Nonsense Guide to Fathering* by Carolyn T. Chubet	$4.95
0681404507	*No Nonsense Guide to Pregnancy Birth and Bonding* by Carolyn T. Chubet	$4.95
0681411538	*Calligraphy For Your Celebrating Your Newborn* by Margaret Shepherd	$5.95

Order by phone with VISA, MasterCard,
American Express or Discover:
☎ **1-800-322-2000**, Dept. 706

or send your order to:

Longmeadow Press, Order/Dept. 706
P.O. Box 305188, Nashville, TN 37230-5188

Name _____

Address _____

City _____ State _____ Zip _____

Item No.	Title	Qty	Total

Check or Money Order enclosed Payable to Longmeadow Press

Charge: ☐ MasterCard ☐ VISA ☐ American Express ☐ Discover

Account Number

☐☐☐☐☐ ☐☐☐☐☐ ☐☐☐☐☐ ☐☐☐☐☐

Card Expires

☐☐☐☐

	Total
Subtotal	
Tax	
Shipping	2.95
Total	

Signature _____ Date _____

Please add your applicable sales tax: AK, DE, MT, MN, OR 0%—CO 3.6%—AL, GA, HI, IA, LA, ME, NE, VT, WY 4%—VA, 4.5%—AR, ID, IN, KS, KY, MA, MD, ME, NC, ND, OH, SC, SD, WI 5%—NM 5.25%—AZ 5.5%—MO 5.75%—DC, FL, MN, MS, NJ, NV, PA, RI, WV 6%—CA, IL, UT 6.25%—NY, OK, TN, TX 7%—WA 7.5%—CT 8%